Using the Telephone More Effectively

Second Edition ◆ Madeline Pascucci Bodin

BARRON'S

DEDICATION

For my husband, Mark

All inquiries should be addressed to:
Barron's Educational Series, Inc.
250 Wireless Boulevard
Hauppauge, New York 11788

Library of Congress Catalog Card No. 97-13910

International Standard Book No. 0-8120-9897-8

Library of Congress Cataloging-in-Publication Data
Bodin, Madeline.
    Using the telephone more effectively / by Madeline Bodin. —
2nd ed.
      p.   cm. — (Barron's business success series)
    Includes index.
    ISBN 0-8120-9897-8
    1. Telephone in business.   I. Title.   II. Series
HF5541.T4B63 1997
651.7'3—dc21   97-13910
                                                       CIP

PRINTED IN HONG KONG
987654321

Contents

◆

Chapter 1

◆

Introduction:

Acquiring More Sophisticated Telephone Skills

"Training is everything. The peach was once a bitter almond; cauliflower is nothing but cabbage with a college education."

—Mark Twain

You already know how to use the telephone. The question is, are you using it effectively? Never has a business technology been so taken for granted. Never has a business technology been used by so many with so little training. No wonder many business people feel that the telephone wastes more time than it saves.

It doesn't have to be that way.

You wouldn't dream of using a new software package without training, or at least looking at the system's on-line tutorial. Yet in the workplace, most people get no additional training in business

telephone skills. Business people are expected to use the telephone—and be effective—using only the social telephone skills they learned as children. As a business person, your communications needs are more sophisticated. Telephone systems have also become more complicated. Let this book be your tutorial.

Have you ever played telephone tag? A few simple tactics can help you cut down on the number of telephone calls it takes for you to reach someone. Did you ever lose a caller while trying to transfer her to another department? Every telephone system works a little differently. Find out who knows the quirks of your company's system. Have you ever wished your company's telephone system had that feature you used at your last company? It probably exists on this system too. Materials from your telephone vendor can help you find the feature and learn how to use it too.

Does your secretary only answer your telephone and take messages? Your secretary can do much more to become a part of your telephone effectiveness team. Have you ever lost out on a big deal because you couldn't reach the correct person in time? Find out how to get the information you need, even when that vital person is not available. Do you know the name of your most important client's secretary? Become friendly with "screeners," and you'll become much more effective on the telephone.

Do you carefully prepare a presentation before you call a client to make a sale? A consultive selling technique can help you make more sales. Have you ever screamed at an irate customer, figuring you had lost their business anyway? Handling customer complaints well can win your company a customer for life.

Have you ever gotten lost in a maze of technology while trying to "Dial one for sales..."? There is a secret to using automated attendants, and those who know it speed right past these devices. Do you just say your name, company name, and telephone number when leaving a voice-mail message? You can be much more effective by leaving a detailed message.

This book will teach you how to

◆ prioritize your return calls so they are all returned in time;

◆ screen your own telephone calls even if you do not have a secretary;

◆ keep telephone calls on track so callers don't waste your time;

◆ get in touch with someone after one telephone message, not dozens;

◆ use the forgotten features of your company's telephone system;

◆ work with your secretary or assistant to keep your phone calls under control;

◆ reach busy or important people by telephone and salvage the call if you can't;

◆ sell products and ideas by telephone;

◆ use the telephone to turn irate customers into faithful customers;

◆ deal with the most dreaded business technology—the automated attendant;

◆ make voice mail work for you, not against you;

◆ prepare for a teleconference or a videoconference.

You have probably outgrown many office skills. For example, you may no longer type your own letters, and someone else may file your reports. You may have delegated your photocopying chores. But you will always need telephone skills. They will take you right to the top.

Chapter 2

◆

Basic Telephone Skills:

What Every Manager Needs to Know

"Speech is power: to persuade, to convert, to compel."

—Ralph Waldo Emerson

The secret to using the telephone effectively is planning. But have you ever planned a telephone call before picking up the receiver? If you answer "no" to this question, don't feel bad. Most business people would answer the same way if they answered truthfully. We love the telephone because it is spontaneous, quick, easy.

Yet how often do business people complain that the telephone is their biggest waste of time? How much of your day is spent on the telephone without getting anything accomplished? A few seconds of planning before you pick up the telephone can make every minute you spend on the telephone more effective.

Most of us learned how to use the telephone as a social skill, not a business skill. The rules differ for business telephone calls. Making a business call requires the same skills as participating in a meeting or writing a memo or business letter. It requires thought and planning.

You can see how you could plan your calls to other people — if you wanted to—but you may not think it is possible to plan for other people's calls to you. It *is* possible, and necessary, to plan for these incoming calls. The first thing to plan is how you will answer your telephone.

The first ten to fifteen seconds of a telephone call set the tone of the entire conversation. As you can imagine, every word of the way you answer the telephone is very important. Business telephone experts agree that you should answer your telephone with a couple of key words that let your callers know they have reached the right place.

Answering your phone with a brusk "What do you want?" will set a negative tone for the conversation that follows. You must answer your phone with a phrase that is both pleasant and professional.

Nancy Friedman, a St. Louis-based communications consultant known as The Telephone "Doctor," says this key phrase should contain three things:

◆ a greeting,

◆ the name of your company or department, and

◆ your name.

"Hello, accounting, this is Lynn Johnson" is a suggested greeting that contains all three elements.

This, of course, is the ideal greeting.

The more frequently you answer your telephone, however, the shorter your greeting will have to be, just for the sake of practicality. If you answer your phone over thirty times a day, you deserve to give your callers a brief greeting or to use a device that will play your greeting to callers. If you answer your phone less than ten times a day, you should be able to be generous with your greeting.

The other factor in deciding exactly how much information to give callers in your greeting is how often you get misdirected calls. If you answer with just your name, you may waste several minutes before you figure out that the person has not even reached the right company. If this happens often, go with the full, information-rich greeting. If it never happens, you can get away with a shorter greeting.

The appropriateness of greetings varies with the type of company you work for, your department, and your personal style. "Hello," "Good morning," or any other salutation that agrees with your personal, departmental, and company image can be used. The exact phrasing and the amount of information you decide to include in your greeting will depend on several things, the most important being how many times a day you answer your telephone. If you answer the phone infrequently, you can use a longer phrase. If your telephone is constantly ringing, try to limit the number of words you use to save your voice and your time.

Friedman says that the greeting also acts as a buffer, that is, it keeps the important information—your department and name—from being clipped from the conversation by speakerphones, long-distance services, or inattentive listeners.

Callers expect to hear a greeting when their call is answered. "Hello" or some other phrase gives your caller a split second to acknowledge that the phone has been answered and to prepare for the information that will follow. Giving a greeting when you answer the phone seems to be the most basic telephone effectiveness skill—after all it is one that is used for social telephoning as well as business use. Yet it is a skill that is often forgotten among business people.

The next time you call someone and immediately get the feeling that he is less than professional, think for a minute. Chances are he either did not use a greeting when answering your call or used one that was impolite or disinterested (for example, "Yeah?" or "Mmm Hmm.").

If you have a direct line or your calls do not pass through a receptionist or secretary, include your company name when you answer your calls. If your calls do pass through a receptionist or secretary, include the name of your department in addition to your own name.

For your name, the phrase "This is Lynn Johnson" is preferred to "Lynn Johnson speaking." Remember that the last thing you say becomes the first thing on the caller's mind.

Another thing to consider in those critical first ten to 15 seconds is your tone of voice. If you are having a bad day, or something is bothering you, put aside your bad mood for at least those first 15 seconds of the call. This will give you enough time to set a positive tone for the conversation. Chances are, if you pay attention to your tone in first 15 seconds, the rest of the call will continue pleasantly with little additional effort on your part.

Another suggestion is an old telemarketer's trick—put a mirror near your telephone to make sure you are creating the right impression. Your body position and facial expression come across on the phone. A mirror makes you aware of your expression—and therefore the impression you are making.

When you make a telephone call, pay attention to what happens in those first 15 seconds. Does the person you have reached sound rushed? Tired? Bored? If they sound rushed and you need several minutes of their time, ask if you can call back at a later time.

Match the speed and tone of your voice to theirs, as long as it fits within the acceptable range for business conversation. The busy business person will appreciate your speaking quickly and not wasting her time. The more laid-back business person will appreciate your slower pace. Of course if the person you call is rude, sleepy, or foolishly chirpy, don't go to those extremes. Be soothing with the rude person (or ask to call back later). Be a bit slower with the sleepy person (but don't nod off yourself) and a bit more upbeat with the chirpy person. But don't mimic their tone of voice, just match it with your own natural voice as best you can.

Listen to the information in the greeting to make sure you have reached the right place. It is amazing how many business calls begin with an informative greeting such as "Hello, accounting department. This is Lynn." It is then followed by "Hi. Is this Bob?" There is no excuse for not listening.

CALL SCREENING AND INTERRUPTIONS

Many business people prefer to have all their calls screened. Your secretary or assistant can screen your calls. If you don't have an assistant or secretary you may do it yourself. *Call screening* has gotten a bad reputation. When we think of call screening, we think of a secretary dedicated to keeping all telephone calls from the boss. But the secretary who takes that approach is not screening calls effectively. "A secretary should screen calls in, not screen calls out," says Dr. Larry Baker, a time-management consultant and president of the Time Management Center—St. Louis. "A secretary should make sure you get all the important calls."

WHEN YOU MUST SCREEN YOUR OWN CALLS

The first thing you should do when answering your own telephone is to quickly and politely find out what the caller wants. A phrase such as "How can I help you?" or "What can I do for you?" quickly brings the caller to the point of the call.

Dr. Baker says that you must compare the importance of each phone call to the importance of the work it is interrupting. If the call is not as important, find another person to help the caller. The idea is not to dump the call on someone else but to find someone who can actually assist the caller.

If you are the only one who can help the caller, ask whether you can call him back later in the day or on another day when you have more time to help. Give a specific time when you will return the call, and consider it an appointment you must keep. If the caller needs your help immediately, set a time limit so that you can get back to your own project quickly. Say something like "I only have ten minutes. Can we discuss this in that time or should I call you back later?"

When you screen your own calls, says Dr. Baker, one of the hardest things to do is to get rid of a total time waster. "You have to be able to say no without guilt," he says. If something is not in your interest or is not your responsibility, you must say so. According to Baker, every phone call you receive can be put into three categories:

◆ I will talk to them now.

◆ I will talk to them later.

◆ The call is not in my interest or area of responsibility.

SETTING PRIORITIES

Dr. Baker's method of placing calls in one of three categories builds on priority-setting skills that are probably second nature to you. It's a helpful formula to use those skills to screen your own calls with minimum interruption to your work.

Dr. Baker made a name for himself as a time-management expert by prioritizing telephone calls (or any other business task) against two yardsticks. He calls those yardsticks "importance" and "urgency," but you can think of them in terms of "if" and "when."

Most people know *if* a call should be handled, but sometimes the urgency (or "when") of the call changes things considerably. For example, the mailroom may call you because your overnight package carrier noticed you didn't specify whether you wanted overnight or two-day delivery for a particular package. Is the call important? Perhaps not, but if you don't handle it immediately, you may lose the opportunity to decide how the package is sent.

When you receive a call, you should ask yourself two questions:

1. Is this call more *important* than what I am doing now?

2. Is this call more *urgent* than what I am doing now?

If you answer "yes" to either question, handle the call immediately. Unfortunately, things are rarely so simple, notes Baker. The call may be equally as important as what you are doing but may need to be handled more quickly. Time-management experts often tell people to set priorities, but don't tell them to look at what's best for the team.

If the call is an internal one, you have to look beyond your own priorities to the priorities of the company. If your work is equally important, but the call needs to be handled more quickly, the company is better off if you cooperate with your caller and put your own work aside for a moment.

But being a team player doesn't mean that you must give in to every interruption. If the call is important but the work you are doing is more time-sensitive, ask your caller to wait. If you ask "May I call you back in thirty minutes?" the caller usually will agree. These are the calls in the I-will-talk-to-them-later category.

Of course, there will be times when both you and your caller are on tight deadlines. If the call is both important and urgent, you will need to take some action. "Never send a caller away empty-handed who has come to you with a legitimate need or request," says Baker. If the caller can't wait for you to return the call at a more convenient time, you may want to pass her on to a co-worker who can help. If no co-worker or other resource can help the caller and her request is both important and urgent, Baker suggests that the most effective time-management technique is to stop what you are doing and help the caller. The most effective decision is the one that benefits the company as a whole.

Some telephone calls are of no benefit to your company. When you receive a request that is a waste of time for you or your company, just refuse to handle the call. "Many people have a hard time handling these phone calls," says Baker. "They don't want to be thought of as rude and feel guilty for saying no. But if you think about it, these calls don't benefit anyone. You should feel guilty if you *don't* say no."

It's rare, though, that you can just say no to a telephone call. If you are a manager, for example, most of the phone calls you receive are important and will require your attention, if not now, then at some future time. Getting into the habit of *categorizing* your calls can help you minimize disruptions.

PRIORITIZE YOUR CALLS

When you know what the caller wants, decide if it is more important than what you were doing before the call. Telephone effectiveness experts point out that there are positive interruptions and negative interruptions. It is possible that any given phone call is more important than the paperwork it interrupts.

Of course, if the call is important, you should take it immediately. But if the task that was interrupted is more important, you have a number of options:

◆ arrange to call the person back,

◆ delegate the call to someone else, or

◆ say "no" to a call that will waste your time.

You or your secretary can arrange to call the person back at a later time. Be sure to get a specific time to return the call when you are both available.

Or, you can delegate the call to someone else. Many calls that wind up at a manager's desk do not require a manager's attention. Nancy Friedman reports that eight out of every ten phone calls she receives can be handled by her assistant.

If you delegate a phone call to your assistant, the assistant should let the caller know that he works closely with you and can take care of the problem or question. The person to whom you delegate the call, whether it is your assistant or someone else in your department, should be able to help the caller. "Don't just dump them on someone who can't help them," says Baker of the Time Management Center.

The third possibility is that the phone call is a total waste of your time. "If the call is not in your interest or responsibility, you have to be able to say no without guilt," says Baker.

LOOK FOR PATTERNS

It may seem that incoming calls are unpredictable, that you can't tell who will call you, when they will call you, or what they will ask about. By keeping a log of your telephone calls, you may find that you are able to predict the volume and nature of calls. You may find that the same people call you about the same things at certain times during the day, week, or month.

For example, you may find that salespeople always call the day after the month's sales figures are released. Or you may find that your clients tend to flood you with inquiries on Monday mornings and complaints on Wednesday afternoons. After you have determined the patterns in the calls you receive, you can arrange your work agenda so that the calls are less disruptive.

TOP TIME SAVERS

Time is important to all managers, but if you must answer and screen your own telephone calls, using your time on the telephone effectively is even more important. Here are some tactics that will help you get the most out of your time on the telephone.

◆ If you know that you will have to wait on hold for a long time, and especially if you are making several calls in a row where you may have a long wait, update your telephone contact information while you wait. Keep a stack of changes near the phone so that you can reach them quickly while on hold. Or, do any other brief, repetitive, menial chore while on hold. Remember to prepare by having the materials you need within reach.

◆ To shorten the amount of time it takes to answer the phone, keep your phone on your left side and keep a paper and pencil on your right nearby. Arrange your desk the opposite way if you are left-handed.

◆ Transcribe your voice-mail messages by writing them on paper or typing them into your computer when you have several of them. Listening to snips of many voice-mail messages to find the correct one is very time-consuming.

◆ If you think that the phone is taking over your life, don't waste time on unproductive chit-chat. You may not realize how often you turn an average two and a half minute business call into a half-hour gab fest. Try sticking to business on most calls and see if the situation improves. (Of course, you wouldn't want to eliminate the vital social element of a business telephone call entirely.)

◆ When you must call someone you know is chatty, call her just before you know she will be leaving—for lunch or for the day.

◆ When returning calls that don't require an answer from the person you are calling, make the calls at lunch. Chances are you will get the person's voice mail.

◆ Don't make telephone calls one at a time. Have a time each day when you make telephone calls. Dial one call right after the other.

◆ During your telephone calling time, put a sign on your door (or cubicle) and ask co-workers not to interrupt during that time. Tell co-workers you will be happy to speak to them after the hour (or other period of time) is up.

One of the biggest wastes of time on the telephone is people who just can't get to the point. There are several ways to steer them back. Ask important questions early on. Interrupt (politely) to ask for pertinent information. If you have to transfer the call, remind the caller that giving you the information you ask for up front will save him from repeating the story later.

Again, if the person is not getting to the point, ask, "How can I help you today?" Remind the caller of your time limit, or set one if you didn't do so at the beginning of the conversation. "I have just ten minutes...." If the purpose of the call is over, wind up by asking if the caller needs more help and then say, "It has been nice speaking with you...."

Chatting with business associates on the telephone makes the workday more pleasant. You probably won't want to eliminate all the social aspects of your business telephone calls. Save the chat for after the business segment of the call. This way, if either party needs to cut the call short, you have already accomplished the goal of your call.

THE MOST IMPORTANT TELEPHONE ACCESSORY

Keep a pen or pencil and a supply of paper near your telephone. "I can't imagine a telephone without paper and a pen nearby," says Nancy Friedman, "but I see it often when I go into other people's offices to make a phone call."

When you receive a telephone call, the first thing you should do is jot down the name of the person who is calling. At first a phonetic spelling of the name will do. If you need to follow up with written material or another call, ask for the precise spelling.

Once you have the caller's name, use it to address her in the course of the conversation. This lets your caller know you are paying attention and care about the call. Of course, you should be careful not to overdo it. You have probably received calls from people who used your name in every sentence, much as an unctuous used car salesman might.

Some companies provide employees with as much scrap paper, taken from the company's recycled white paper, as they need. Other companies provide printed pads or other new stationery that you may not feel comfortable using for sketchy telephone notes. One option is to use the back side of your old business cards. This lets you put the notes from one call on one piece of paper. Chances are that most of these note cards will wind up right in the trash. If you need to save the notes, either pop the card into your file, or transcribe your rough notes into a form that is more useful to you.

These days many people who use the telephone frequently also use software to help them keep track of their telephone contacts. Some people (especially those who don't touch type) find it difficult to take notes on their computers while they are speaking on the telephone. A simple solution is to take notes with the paper and pen you keep right near your telephone and transcribe those notes into your computer software when the conversation is finished.

We'll talk more about the benefits of using one of these software products in Chapter 10. If you don't use contact management software, consider keeping a notebook next to your telephone. Use the notebook to log each call—incoming and outgoing. Note the date, time, person you spoke with, and subject of the call. You may even want to take your rough notes here. After some time, calling patterns (inquiries on Monday, salespeople at the end of the month) should become apparent.

KEEPING DISORGANIZED CALLERS ON TRACK

When you receive a call, you may have a tendency to be a passive recipient of information. After you get into the habit of taking notes, you will find that jotting down a few key words or phrases will help you keep the conversation on track if the caller digresses.

And these notes also serve as reminders of what was discussed when the call ends.

Sometimes a disorganized caller will make you disorganized. If there is certain information you need to help callers with common questions (for example, department codes to requisition materials or invoice numbers to track accounts payable), make a list for yourself to make sure that you get all the information you need from a disorganized caller. Airline reservation agents are particularly good at this, says Baker. They get callers to give information in the order it is needed.

RECAP EACH CONVERSATION

Still, the details of a conversation become vague soon after the discussion ends. At the end of your conversation, therefore, quickly summarize what was said and decided. It is unnatural to recap a conversation, but you should be secure enough to do it. If it's worth discussing at length, it's worth a thirty-second recap. The wrap-up allows both parties to come away with a clear picture of the purpose of the call and what was accomplished.

The most important thing that should come out of this recap is the action each of you will take next. "I will send you the minutes of the meeting." "I will wait for your next call." "I will cut the check." Don't let a telephone conversation end without knowing what you must do and what the other person plans to do next.

WHEN YOU MUST ANSWER A CO-WORKER'S PHONE

Let's say that you are walking down the hallway when you hear a telephone ringing and ringing and ringing. You know good business telephone skills require telephone calls to be answered promptly, but you don't know where your co-worker is. At times like this, you may have to answer a co-worker's telephone—even if it is not usually in your job description. (We'll talk about tips for people who answer other people's phones in Chapter 4.)

When you pick up someone else's phone, greet the caller with that person's name as well as your own. For example, you might say, "Hello. Lynn Jones's office. This is Lee Brown." (Of course, some callers will object to speaking to an office, but this is the best way to phrase this complicated answering scenario.)

Offer to take a message or to help the caller if you can. Do not try to answer questions when you don't have answers. Some issues, such as product release dates or marketing strategies, are common knowledge within a company but cannot be given to callers outside the company. If you are answering a call for a co-worker in another department where you don't know the policies, limit your assistance to taking a message. Explain to the caller that you don't normally work closely with the person he is trying to reach. Offer again to take a message. Remember to get the caller's name, company name, phone number (including area code and extension), and some information on what the call is about. After you have taken a message, be sure your co-worker receives it.

Thanks to the popularity of voice mail, the problem of business telephones ringing off the hook and the necessity of answering a co-worker's telephone is no longer common. If the voice-mail system breaks, though, you will know what to do.

RETURNING CALLS

An important part of using the telephone effectively is returning calls. "When you ask a person to leave a message in voice mail or on an answering machine, there is an implied promise that you will return the call," says Baker of the Time Management Center. And when your secretary takes a message, she usually assures the caller you will return the call.

Failure to return the call breaks that real or implied promise, and this doesn't reflect well on you. If you can't return the call yourself, delegate it to a member of your staff who can. If time is the issue, call back to set a date and time for a longer conversation. If there is any possibility that you won't be able to return the call, the best course of action is not to promise to return it in the first place, says Baker.

Although you will find no rule cast in stone, most people expect business telephone messages to be returned within twenty-four hours. If you can't meet this deadline, and no one else can handle the call for you, it is perfectly acceptable, even preferable, to have a secretary or assistant call back, explain the delay, and tell the person when you plan to return the call. If you don't have an assistant, call yourself, explain quickly that you don't have time for anything more than the briefest conversation now, and make an appointment to call back later.

OUTGOING CALLS

Planning the calls you make to other people is easy. After all, you determine the time, nature, and duration of these calls. But making the conversation a productive one—not only for yourself, but for the person you are calling—is another matter.

One way to make productive calls is to be considerate of the time constraints of the people you call. What to you is a quick question in the course of the task at hand may be a needless interruption to the person you are calling.

There are several ways to avoid this problem. You can save up several points that are not urgent and make a single telephone call. But there may be a person that you must speak to several times a day by telephone, even after you have saved up several points. You may want to schedule a few times each day for calls to and from this person so that you are not constantly interrupting each other, suggests Baker.

It's important that both of you make impromptu calls for urgent matters, but saving the merely important matters for your scheduled calls cuts down on interruptions for both of you.

You need not make an elaborate plan for your outgoing calls. Nancy Friedman suggests jotting down six or eight words that will remind you of what you need to accomplish and keep you on track.

SET THE AGENDA

"When you reach someone by phone, you are having a two-person meeting," says Dr. Larry Baker. "Any meeting is more effective with an agenda." It is the caller's responsibility to set the agenda for the telephone call. Having a list of what you want to accomplish along with an awareness of the urgency of each point helps you prepare for the inevitable: that the person you are calling will not be there.

For example, before you call a colleague, you should write a few key words on a piece of paper: "Mortimer contract, northwest region, VP dinner." These words are your agenda for a call in which you want to discuss your company's contract with the Mortimer Company, your company's expansion into the northwestern United States, and the upcoming retirement dinner for the vice president of finance. With this list, you will be able to keep the call on track.

If you have never called the person before, don't start the conversation by asking, "How are you?" Many telephone salespeople consider this to be a good way to warm up a "cold-call," but they have overused the technique so much that when you ask a total stranger how they are, they automatically think you are going to sell them something.

To warm up a business telephone conversation with someone you don't know, ask if you have chosen a good time to talk. This will show your respect for the person's time and should get the call off to a good start.

TIPS ON AVOIDING TELEPHONE TAG

Nancy Friedman estimates that seven out of every ten calls you make are not completed, that is you don't reach the person you are trying to call.

At the very least, what you should get out of any telephone call is the time the person you are trying to reach will return or the best time to call back. "The person you ask will probably say they don't know," says Friedman. "Ask them to make a blind guess. They may tell you the person usually picks up messages at 4:30. At least you will have an idea." Also, always leave a message and make sure your message specifies a time for the person to call you back. If you will be in a meeting until noon, leave that in the message. If you know you are available for only two hours that day, one in the morning and one in the afternoon, let the person you are calling know when you will be available.

Leaving specific messages that include what time is best to return your call helps eliminate *telephone tag*, the office "game" where two people take turns leaving messages for each other.

◆ If the person you are calling has voice mail, leave a message that includes the points on your agenda. If you need the answer to a particular question by a certain time, include that in your message as well. Based on our agenda-setting example, if your colleague was not available, you could leave a voice-mail message that says, "I need to speak to you about the Mortimer contract by five o'clock today, and we also need to discuss northwest regional expansion and Terry's retirement dinner."

◆ Whenever you leave a message, but especially on voice mail, be sure to include your telephone number. Voice-mail systems let people pick up their messages when they are out of the office, and even though your phone number may be in their files, they won't have the files on hand to call you back immediately.

◆ When you reach someone on the first try, respect their time. Estimate how long the conversation will last, and ask them if they have the time to speak to you immediately. And don't hesitate to set up an appointment to speak at a later time. When people don't want to talk to you, you don't want to talk to them. If they are in a rush, you will not have a productive conversation.

◆ When you set up the appointment, make sure that the person knows how urgent the conversation is. If you need an answer to a question by Tuesday, he may be willing to clear some time for you on Monday. If you don't let the person know about your deadline, he may tell you that he is not free until Thursday afternoon.

Impromptu calls are best left for emergencies and social situations. A little bit of planning—jotting down the important points that need to be covered during a call, setting a specific time for telephone call-backs, and leaving detailed messages—helps you get much more out of each telephone call.

YOUR VOICE

Telemarketers know that their voices are their most important sales tool. Telemarketing experts have tons of tips to help telemarketers always sound their best on the telephone. For example, we've already discussed one of the telemarketer's all-time favorite tips: using a mirror before or during a telephone call. Check the mirror to make sure that you are smiling. (If you generally don't smile when meeting with clients or fellow employees, make sure you have "on" the face you would like them to see.)

The best way to improve the quality of your voice over the telephone is to tape yourself during a telephone call. You can use a suction cup device that attaches a microphone to your telephone handset. It's available from electronics stores for just a few dollars. Or you can use an "in-line" recording device that attaches onto your handset cord. These devices are a little more expensive. Or you can just set up a tape recorder on your desk because you are interested in only your side of the conversation anyway.

Keep in mind that laws about taping telephone calls vary from state to state. Some states have very strict laws; other states have no specific laws. But there are still federal regulations to worry about. To be on the safe side of the law, ask the other party before you tape ANY phone conversation. With a little planning, you can get their agreement on tape too. If you have any questions, please consult your company's legal department or your own lawyer.

When you have the tape, listen to it. Most people find it difficult to listen to themselves on tape but force yourself to pay attention.

◆ Do you use filler words like, "Um," "Uh," "Like," "Okay," or "Right"?

◆ Does your voice sound nasal (too much sound is passing through your nose, giving a whiny sound) or like you have a cold (no sound is passing through your nose)?

◆ Do you speak too quickly? Do your words run together? Or do you speak too slowly? (This is a much less common problem.)

◆ Do you pronounce each word clearly, or do you mumble?

◆ Do you sound sleepy, angry, bored?

Chances are, the first time you tape yourself, you won't like what you hear. Don't blame the quality of the recording or the quality of the telephone line. Work on the problems you hear. It takes a lot of practice. After you have practiced, tape yourself again. This time you may be pleased. Tape yourself regularly to make sure your improvements stick and that you haven't picked up any other bad voice habits.

THEY CAN HEAR YOU SLOUCH

Many of the corrections to the way you sound on the telephone can be made by changing the way you look on the telephone. As already mentioned, people on the other end of the phone line can hear you smile, but that's not all they can hear.

Would you ever walk into a face-to-face meeting, put your head on the table and conduct business that way? Never! But if you look around the office you will see all sorts of odd postures when your co-workers are on the phone. That guy's got his feet up on the desk and is reclining in his chair, looking at the ceiling as he talks. That woman is grimacing as she is trying to pull a folder out of a tight drawer as she speaks. That other woman is resting her head in her hand. Are you guilty of any of these phone postures too?

When you are on the telephone, pretend that the person you are talking to is sitting right in front of you. Sit up straight, put your feet on the floor, and look straight ahead. They can hear how you are sitting.

Even cradling the telephone between your shoulder and your ear can strain your voice so much that it can be heard on the other end. Use a headset to make it easier to keep your neck straight while taking notes.

TIPS FOR HEAVY TELEPHONE USERS

If you make or take more than thirty calls a day, you are a heavy telephone user. You are not alone. Millions of Americans work in telephone sales, customer service, technical support, and telephone order departments where they also make or answer dozens of calls each day. Here are some of the things they do to make every call effective, even when they have been on the phone all day. Some of these tactics are sure to work for you too.

◆ Take a break from the phones. Set aside some time each day to complete paperwork, attend meetings, and focus on other aspects of your job. During that time, have someone else handle your calls or forward them to your voice-mail system.

◆ Take mini-breaks every half hour or so. Stretch your neck and shoulders, flex your fingers, and walk around.

◆ Use a headset. A headset and other telephone technologies can make your job easier. We'll talk more about these technologies in Chapter 10.

◆ Make sure that you have plenty to drink (water, juice, soda, herbal tea) nearby. Talking can dry your mouth and throat, as can the stress of handling customer problems. Take frequent sips. Be wary of coffee, tea, and soda with caffeine though. They cause your body to lose some water. Drink them only occasionally.

◆ Group outgoing calls together. Dial them one after another without giving yourself time to procrastinate. Gather all the materials you need for all your calls before you dial the first one.

◆ Review the day's performance. How can you use the telephone more effectively tomorrow?

LOOKING AT THE BIG PICTURE

The basic telephone skills you have learned in this chapter are the building blocks of telephone effectiveness. Answering calls with a key phrase that contains a greeting, your department, and your name will help all the calls you receive go more smoothly. Learning to set the tone of a telephone conversation in the first 15 seconds is also helpful for all calls but will be especially important when you need to make a persuasive or sales call.

Getting into the habit of setting an agenda for the phone calls you make—even if it's just a few words jotted on a piece of paper—will guarantee that you always cover all the points you planned during your call and will save you from making a second phone call. Later, when we discuss voice mail and teleconferencing, we'll see how this skill will help you use these two new telephone technologies better.

Scheduling return telephone calls and asking secretaries and co-workers for information concerning the person you are calling can save time even on routine telephone calls. When you are trying to reach someone who is very busy or important, these skills are crucial.

Although these skills are basic, don't let their simplicity fool you. Turning these skills into habits is not easy. However, if you do, they will help you accomplish more on every call.

Chapter 3

Getting to Know Your Phone System:

The More You Know, the Better

"We live in a time of such rapid change and growth of knowledge that only he who continues to learn and inquire can hope to keep pace, let alone play the role of guide."

—Nathan Pussey (educator)

On your first day of work at a new company, you may get a packet that explains your benefits, describes the company's vacation policy, and lists company holidays. You may get a tour of the office and meet your co-workers. And, if you are lucky, you may get an orientation to the company telephone system. You will no doubt be tempted to skip the phone orientation. After all, you say to yourself, I know how to use a telephone, and there is important work to do.

Learning your new company's phone system is every bit as important as learning the company's policies and procedures. You may know how to put someone on hold, but do you know how the phone system handles a call that has been put on hold? Some systems are programmed to return the call to the company receptionist. Other systems may transfer the call to your secretary, or your phone may ring to remind you that the call is still on hold.

Avail yourself of any telephone training that is offered, whether it is when you start your employment or when a new phone system is installed. Even if you know the basics, you may pick up tips and techniques that will enable you to use familiar features better. Or you may learn about new features or programmable options that will save you time and effort.

What if your company does not offer telephone training? You can use several different resources to find out more about your phone system. The first is the telephone *user's guide*, a single sheet of paper or a card—a crib sheet—on using the most common features of the phone system. A user's guide will help you through those first months with a new phone system and will help new members of your department get up to speed more quickly in the future.

If a user's guide was not included in your new company's orientation packet and your predecessor did not leave a copy in a desk drawer or tacked on a bulletin board, ask one of your co-workers for a copy. If a guide does not exist, create one of your own after doing a little research. (The answers to the questions that follow will create an effective user's guide.)

Don't depend on your co-workers alone when creating your user's guide. Find out who is in charge of your company's telephone system. Large companies may have a telecommunications department to manage the telephone system or a training department that handles all types of employee education. Smaller companies may put the purchasing department, the personnel department, or the office manager in charge of the phone system.

At a large company without established aids for learning the phone system, getting information may be a matter of asking the experts in the telecommunications department and perhaps reading the booklets and manuals they suggest. At a small company you may find yourself reading the system administrator's manual and speaking to the company that sold and installed the phone system.

FINDING OUT ABOUT THE FEATURES

How can you find out about your company's telephone system? Start by asking these questions about the most common phone system features. The answers to these questions vary from system to system. There are even differences from company to company with the same model phone system. Each company customizes the phone system for its own use. You can use the answers to these questions to create a thorough telephone user's manual for yourself or your department.

HOLD

◆ Will the system "time out" on held calls and transfer the held call somewhere else?

◆ How long can someone be left on hold before the system times out?

◆ If a held call is transferred, where does it go?

◆ If you are on one line and don't answer your other line, what happens to the second call? Does it return to the company receptionist? Your secretary or assistant?

TRANSFER

◆ What happens if you transfer a call to another extension and no one answers that extension? Will the phone just ring? Will the call return to you? Will it return to the company receptionist?

◆ Is there any indication that a call has been transferred from within the company?

◆ If there is no answer at the other extension when you transfer a call, can you retrieve the call? How can you do that?

◆ Does the phone system let you have a three-way conference with the person you are transferring and the person you are transferring them to so that you can announce the call?

CONFERENCE

◆ How many parties can participate in one teleconference? How many people inside your company? How many outside? (There will be different numbers for each.)

◆ Can you conference two outside callers together and then drop out of their conversation?

◆ When two people are on hold waiting for more parties to be added to a conference call, can they speak to each other?

◆ How do you get back to the conference call if one of the parties you are trying to add does not answer his phone or is unavailable? (For more information on conference calls, see Chapter 9.)

SPEED DIAL

◆ Does the system have speed-dial numbers that are system wide? How many? How many digits can the system hold for each number?

◆ Does the system have group speed dial—numbers in common for your department? Can system speed dial numbers be set aside for department use?

◆ How do you access speed dial numbers? Are there dedicated buttons on your telephone? An access code? Both?

◆ How many numbers can you have on your personal dial list?

SPEAKERPHONE

◆ How is the speaker turned on and off during a phone call?

◆ Does the system let secretaries and co-workers use the speaker to "voice announce" a call before they transfer it?

◆ Is there a mute button so that callers on voice announce can't hear what is going on in your office?

FORWARD

◆ Is the system programmed to automatically transfer calls if they are not answered?

◆ Can internal and external calls be routed differently?

◆ How are the calls in your department routed?

◆ Can you forward your calls to voice mail? How is that done?

◆ Can your secretary override your call forward and transfer screened calls to you?

◆ How will the system remind you that your calls have been forwarded? Is there a visual indication? An audible one?

Modern phone systems have dozens of features. As you learn about the basic features, ask questions about the more advanced ones. With so many features available, the time-saving feature of your dreams may be waiting for you to discover it. Have you ever wished to be alerted when a busy extension is free without having to stay on the line? That feature is available (for internal calls only) on many phone systems.

USING THE MOST HELPFUL FEATURES

HOLD

Hold is the most basic feature on any business telephone system. You already know how to use it, but here are two things to keep in mind:

◆ Time passes slowly for the caller on hold. Don't leave callers on hold for more than a few seconds without checking on them.

◆ There is nothing wrong with calling someone back. It's more polite to call someone back than to put him or her on hold for several minutes.

TRANSFER

Most phone systems let you blindly transfer calls to another party without checking to see if that party is in. Don't do it. Many phone systems will let you transfer the call and stay on the line to announce the call. Don't expect the caller to start from the beginning with the new person. Explain what has already been said and why you are transferring the call. If your phone system allows you to speak confidentially before the caller is connected, warn your co-worker about other special problems—if the caller has been difficult, for example.

For very important calls, set up a brief conference call among the three parties to make introductions and ensure that the transfer goes smoothly.

SPEED DIAL

Most people know how to use speed dial to store frequently dialed numbers. But many people don't realize that speed dial has other uses as well. For example, your telephone has several feature buttons, such as hold and transfer. You use other features by dialing a code. You can program a speed-dial button with the feature access code of a feature you use frequently and have one button access to that feature. Or, you can enter the country and city code for overseas cities you call frequently, which saves you time dialing all calls to that locality.

Even though speed dial is a handy place to store access codes, don't put personal I.D. numbers or other security numbers on your speed dial. Not only can anyone with access to your phone now access the secure system, but your phone probably has an LCD screen that displays the security number when someone presses the speed-dial button. Anyone can copy this number from your display and use it later to access the system.

CALL FORWARD

Call forward allows you to forward your calls to someone who can handle them. It is especially useful if your responsibilities involve dealing with customers. At the very least, brief the person your calls are forwarded to on the information you need to have before you return the call.

And don't forget to take your phone off call forward when you don't need it. "You would be surprised how many calls for telephone repair are caused by people who left their call forward on and forgot about it," says one telephone consultant. To avoid that problem, some companies ask their receptionist to clean the system of forwarded calls once a week.

The most important step you can take to learn how to use your company's telephone system effectively is to make an effort to learn about it. Attend training sessions. Read the manual or users' guide. Track down the manual yourself if it is not immediately available.

A few minutes of learning to use your telephone will pay for itself in years of more knowledgeable and effective telephone use.

Chapter 4

The Telephone Effectiveness Team—You and Your Secretary:

*Working Together Can Make You
More Productive*

"The tree is known by its fruit."

—Matthew 12:33

If you are lucky enough to have a secretary or an assistant, you can be a far more effective user of the telephone. A secretary or assistant can screen your calls to make sure important calls get through to you and unnecessary calls do not interrupt your work. A secretary can also *organize* your messages and make sure you have the information you need before making or returning calls.

Even a good secretary or assistant needs input and cooperation from you to make the system work to your benefit. It is up to you to set the guidelines that will enable you and your assistants to work together as an efficient telephone team.

THE BASICS (AGAIN)

All the basic telephone skills that apply to you, apply to your secretary too. For many callers, your secretary provides the first, and perhaps only, impression callers have of you. The conversation should reflect well on your abilities as a manager and a business person.

Everyone who answers the telephone in your company should be prepared to take telephone messages or direct calls as needed. They should be able to do this professionally, reflecting well on your company. This applies to executives as well as temps in the mailroom.

You probably can't do anything about the telephone-handling skills of your company's executives, or the folks in the mailroom, but you can make sure that you, your secretary, and any other employees under your supervision know how to use the telephone effectively.

Your secretary or assistant's greeting should be professional and enthusiastic. Like your greeting, it should reflect where this call falls in the chain of events that gets the caller to you. If callers can reach your secretary directly, the greeting should include your company name. If the call was first directed by a company receptionist, the company name can be omitted.

If your secretary answers all calls in your department, the department name should be mentioned. ("Hello, marketing department, this is Terry.") If you have a personal secretary, the greeting should include your name too. Now if you have a direct-dial number answered by a personal secretary, the greeting could be quite a mouthful. Keep it as brief as possible, but tell your secretary to take a deep breath and don't rush. It's okay to take a (short) breath somewhere in the middle if required. Telephone greetings always sound longer when the person giving them is trying to speed through them at a breakneck clip.

Here's an example of a greeting for a telephone number that rings directly to your office without first going to a company receptionist and is answered by your personal secretary. "Hello. This is the Big Company, Lynn Johnson's office. I'm Terry."

If you find your telephone greeting too taxing for your secretary (or yourself), consider purchasing a personal announcement system. This gizmo answers calls with a brief, digitally recorded announcement and then turns the call over to the person who answered it. The message can be rerecorded everyday to match your secretary's voice exactly. Most people never realize a machine is involved with the call. We'll talk more about these gizmos in Chapter 10.

To offer a professional greeting, your secretary must sound professional. Gum, if chewed, should be safely tucked away when answering the phone. Snacks should not be crunched either. There should be no gum cracking or lip smacking in the caller's ear.

Your secretary should sound friendly. The easiest way to do this is to smile before picking up the phone. The experts swear that you can hear a smile over the telephone.

Nancy Friedman calls the tone that all business people, but especially secretaries, should adopt, "business friendly." (She's even registered the term as a trademark.) What it means is answering callers not in a formal, cold, and aloof way, but in a warmer, caring, but still business-like way.

The keys to maintaining a "business friendly" tone involve treating each call as unique, showing empathy, trying to solve problems without arguing, and, of course, smiling while you talk.

CALL SCREENING

Effective call screening lets you get important work done without interruption from unimportant calls. Ineffective call screening alienates your callers and may even keep important calls from reaching you. According to time-management consultant Dr. Larry Baker, the most important factor in call screening is the attitude of the secretary. "The secretary must screen calls in, not screen calls out," he says. "Don't take a negative approach to screening calls. Secretaries who think their job is to screen out calls that will interrupt their bosses have the wrong attitude. The secretary must think about making sure the boss gets the calls that are important."

Imagine what would happen if a member of your company's board of directors called your office, and your secretary, hearing an unfamiliar name, said you were unavailable. Because your secretary was screening *out* unfamiliar names instead of screening *in* important calls, you do not get the call, and probably make the board member angry.

Every secretary should be provided with a list of VIPs. This list can be broken down to differentiate between those who should be put through no matter what and those who should be put through if you are not in a meeting or rushing to beat a deadline. Your VIP list should include your boss's name and the names of all upper-level management. Also list your personal VIPs—including your husband or wife and your children. This helps spare your loved ones the annoyance of being screened, and it may also save your secretary considerable embarrassment.

Your secretary should also have a list of people to screen out. Make it clear that every caller should be dealt with in a polite and professional manner but that certain individuals must wait until you have time for them.

Tell your secretary how to deal with salespeople. Do you want to see written materials before you speak to them? Will you call them back at a later time? Should they be referred to the purchasing department?

Make sure your secretary knows routine information:

◆ your fax number,

◆ the company address,

◆ the names of people in charge of purchasing and personnel,

◆ the name of your boss and your boss's boss,

◆ special procedures,

◆ subjects that can be handled by a staff member or another department, and

◆ the names of contacts at those other departments.

Each phone call your secretary handles is another call that won't interrupt you. However, you may want to give out certain information yourself, even if it can be handled by your secretary. For example, if you are trying to get a feel for the audience attending a seminar or a speech, you may want to take some of the calls yourself. Your secretary could handle the RSVPs, because the calls will mostly consist of clerical tasks—checking off lists, recording names and addresses, and so on. But if you handle a few calls yourself, you will have the opportunity to speak to some of the attendees before the event and ask them questions. Doing so may give you a feel for your audience or the effectiveness of the invitations.

Call screening and the phrase "May I tell her who is calling?" are so common in the business world that few people object to them. Callers who are confident that they have something to offer are also confident that they will get through your screen.

Some people will object to call screening. Most managers have their secretaries put through these difficult callers so that they don't accidentally insult a major client or other VIP. Be sure your secretary knows what to do when a caller won't give his name.

If you are unavailable to everyone—if you are in a meeting, out of the office, or entertaining a visitor, for example—have your secretary state this before asking for the name of the caller. Callers appreciate not being screened, and if your secretary offers to pull you out of a meeting after hearing a VIP's name, you have made it clear how important that caller is to you.

Don't give your secretary a script to read. Pat responses can't effectively screen callers. Your goal is to give your secretary the tools and skills needed to handle all types of calls. When call screening is a process, and not just a reading of a script, unusual calls can be screened as efficiently as routine calls.

TAKING MESSAGES

A standard while-you-were-out pad is sufficient for taking messages—as long as the message is complete. If you need special information to return phone calls productively, you can design your own form and have it made into a pad. However, keep in mind that secretaries often have a hard enough time pulling enough information out of callers to complete even short message forms. Busy callers don't always have the patience to spell out their names and leave phone numbers, let alone answer other questions.

Ideally every phone message should include

◆ the caller's name,

◆ the company name, and

◆ the telephone number, including the area code and an extension.

Instruct your secretary to prompt callers for this information if necessary.

Many callers rush through their messages and hang up before the information can be checked. Therefore, have your secretary read back spellings and phone numbers letter by letter and number by number as the caller goes along. It is also helpful to know the nature of the call, but often the message is too complicated to transcribe in a short amount of time. A quick phrase from the caller ("I want to reschedule our lunch") and a few words on the message pad ("Re: rescheduling lunch") can save valuable time for everyone in the long run.

Have your secretary arrange your phone messages in order of importance. This saves you the trouble of picking through them, trying to figure out what is important. Telemarketers have found that they place phone calls more quickly if they don't have to decide which to make first but can just dial through a stack of messages.

Also ask your secretary to gather materials pertinent to your messages. If the call concerns a letter, for example, have your secretary retrieve it from your correspondence file and clip it to the message. If customer records will make the call-back more productive, have your secretary retrieve the file containing those records.

HANDLING RINGING PHONES

Things sometimes get hectic, but phones should never ring off the hook with no one answering them. Few things make a worse impression on a caller than having a call go unanswered during business hours. You should arrange for someone to cover your phone when both you and your secretary are unavailable.

You may also want to set a policy at the department level for ringing phones. People use customer service to differentiate between companies, and companies need every edge they can get over their competitors. Customer service is everyone's business, and whenever the phone rings it's a "customer." Even internal calls represent a kind of customer.

The most important thing a manager can do to ensure that calls are answered promptly is to *set a policy* and put it in writing. The policy should outline tiers of telephone answerers and specify the number of rings after which the phone will be answered by the next tier. The call can be automatically routed by your telephone system to the next tier after a certain number of rings, or someone in a neighboring office may simply pick up the ringing telephone.

For example, your company policy may state that, if a staff member's telephone rings more than three times, it will be answered by the departmental secretary. If it is not answered after four rings (because the departmental secretary is not available), it should be answered by the staff member's nearest neighbor. And at a certain point (five or six rings) anyone who hears the phone ringing should answer it.

As a general rule, people expect business telephones to be answered in no more than four rings. Some managers and companies have a strict four-ring policy: pick up the phone by the fourth ring—or else. Although this works in certain corporate cultures, assigning responsibility for ringing phones usually gets the job done.

Answering other people's telephones benefits the team. When other staff members answer calls, the efficiency of the whole department is improved. If a staff member says, "That's not my call; that's not my job," remind her that everyone is on the same team.

If you have a private line, don't forget to include it when setting the telephone-answering policy for the department. Often your private line isn't automatically routed to another phone if you don't answer it. Because your most important calls may be coming over this line, it is especially important that your secretary, assistant, or other staff members know how these calls should be handled.

Today's technology leaves no excuse for telephones that are not answered. If, after setting an answering policy, your department's phones are still ringing off the hook, consider getting a voice-mail system.

COVERING THE PHONES AT LUNCH

When more than one secretary or assistant is in a department, it is very common to have the assistants take shifts to make sure callers can reach a live person while most of the department is at lunch. A simple way to accomplish this is to make up a schedule and have one assistant cover noon to 1 P.M. and another cover 1 P.M. to 2 P.M.

In some departments the telemarketer's "tennis ball" technique can work too. Have on hand as many tennis balls or other symbolic objects as people you need to cover the telephones at lunch. The person who has the tennis ball on his desk is the person who is responsible for answering the telephones. When that person goes to lunch, he hands off the tennis ball to another assistant. If there is no one to hand the tennis ball off to, the assistant with the ball has to stick around until someone comes back.

If you have a responsible department that works well together, this technique can make lunch-time coverage work to everyone's advantage. But if you have a problem with assistants taking long lunches or if the assistants just don't play fair, you should avoid this technique.

VOICE MAIL AND YOUR SECRETARY

These days it seems that most companies have already gone the voice-mail route. Voice mail means the end to endlessly ringing phones and lost while-you-were-out slips, but it brings its own set of problems. We'll cover the solutions to these problems in Chapter 8. If you are lucky enough to have both a voice-mail system and a secretary, you can do a few things to make sure your whole telephone support team, human and electronic, is working to make things easier for you and your callers.

First, most voice-mail systems give callers an "out" from your voice-mail greeting. Some let callers press zero to be transferred back to the company receptionist, to a departmental secretary, or to your personal secretary. Other systems let callers dial any other extension to try to reach a live person.

Be sure to mention the most effective option in your voice-mail greeting. Give your callers the name of the person they will be speaking to, if possible. For example, "If you need to speak to a live person, please dial extension 330 now to speak to Mary." If your only option is to have the callers press zero and go back to a bank of company telephone receptionists, don't give a specific name because they may wind up with someone else.

It is possible to have your secretary listen to your voice-mail messages for you and write down the messages on a piece of paper, or a message slip, for your attention later. Even though this may give you an extra hand in prioritizing your call-backs, most people listen to their own voice-mail messages. In fact, callers expect only you to listen to your voice-mail messages. If someone else routinely sorts them for you, you may want to alert your callers to this in your greeting.

If you need to forward voice-mail messages left for you to your secretary, don't forget to add a brief message of your own. The message itself may not make it clear that it was originally sent to you. (Not everyone starts their message with your name.) Give your secretary instructions on what to do with the message. Should she call back for more information? Send the information requested?

Sometimes the action that should be taken isn't clear from the message itself. A brief attachment to each forwarded message will ensure that the correct action is taken.

If you will be out of the office for more than a few days, you should include the name and extension of a co-worker, secretary, or assistant in your greeting. Do this even if you normally handle all your calls yourself, or if you are retrieving your voice-mail messages while you are away. Callers like to know that they can reach someone immediately if possible, and lengthy meetings, traffic, or an airplane delay can keep you from checking your messages yourself.

The important thing here is to make sure that the person you are using as your emergency back-up knows about his role and acts accordingly. Callers should not hear your message, dial another extension, and then hear another message asking them to dial a third person, only to get a message from the third person that says she is not available. It happens more often than you think.

Choose a person as your back-up who will be in the office the entire time you are gone. If your secretary will be taking a few days off while you are away, she is not a good choice. Ask your back-up to have someone answer her phone when she is away from her desk. If this is not possible, ask your back-up to return calls forwarded from your extension promptly. Ask her to create a voice-mail greeting that mentions your name and explains the situation.

For example, "Hello, this is Terry Smith. I am away from my desk right now. If you are calling for Lynn Johnson and need immediate assistance, please leave a message for me and I will return your call within the hour...."

HIRING TELEPHONE PERSONNEL

If your secretary will spend most of his time on the telephone, or if you are hiring other staff primarily for telephone work, use some of the tricks telemarketers use to make sure that you find people who are well suited for telephone work.

First, do your initial interview by telephone. If you have many openings, you may want to screen candidates through voice mail. Have a special voice-mail mailbox set up for applicants' replies. In the voice-mail greeting, ask two to four questions. The candidates' responses will tell you how well they listen, how well they think on their feet, their basic telephone demeanor, and, of course, the basic information you asked in your questions.

If the job is entirely a telephone position, don't let the person's appearance sway you regarding their telephone skills. Attractive telephone voices don't necessarily come attached to attractive faces or bodies.

Second, give your new hires the training needed for a basic telephone task. Then let them perform that task and provide more training gradually. Some telephone sales and customer service positions require months of expensive training before a new hire can handle the full range of calls. The time to find out whether a new hire can't cut it on the telephone is before you spend the time and money training her, not after months of work.

HAVING YOUR SECRETARY PLACE CALLS FOR YOU

"It is not unprofessional to have a secretary place a call for you," says Dr. Baker, "but it is unprofessional not to be on the phone within five or six seconds." If you are having a difficult time reaching someone, having your secretary place the call for you can save time. But you must be ready to speak to the person immediately when the call is put through.

Keeping the person you called waiting implies, even if you don't intend it to, that your time is much more valuable than their time. Getting on the phone promptly shows the consideration necessary for a productive phone conversation.

When you receive a call placed by a secretary, expect to be connected to the caller within five or six seconds. If you refuse to wait at all, you come across as unprofessional, says Dr. Baker, but it is up to you to set the limit on how long you will wait. He thinks that twenty seconds is a reasonable limit to set—but that is a generous limit, and you may find that it is too long. Respecting other people's time and being sure your own is respected is one of the keys to greater telephone effectiveness.

Chapter 5

How to Get in Touch with Anyone by Phone:

Suggestions on How to Reach Your Goals

"The secret of success is constancy to purpose."
—Benjamin Disraeli

When you make a business call, there is usually a good reason for it. You may want to deliver a message, need information, or hope to buy or sell something. If the person you are calling is difficult to reach, you may get frustrated and lose sight of the reason for the call. When this happens, it may be helpful to focus on the goal of your call. Contacting an individual is merely the means to reaching that goal.

The point of a business call is *rarely* simply to speak with someone. A business call may have a social aspect. For instance, you may call a client to say hello, to ask how things are, or to "touch base." Usually a business call has a *goal*. The goal may be to get information, to deliver information such as the time of a meeting, or to sell a product.

Before you make a telephone call, you should have a clear idea of what you want to accomplish with that call. If you suspect that it will be difficult to reach the person or if your calls are not being returned, you must sit down and separate what you *want* to accomplish from what you *need*.

You may want to call up the CEO of a Fortune 500 company, impress him with your sales acumen, and not only sell him millions of dollars' worth of your product but also have your name on his lips for the next two months as the best salesperson in the business.

In reality, if you need to sell a product to a Fortune 500 company, you will be stonewalled if you start with the CEO. It is easy to be led off track by pursuing an industry leader or someone with a prestigious title. That is why it is important to keep the goal of your phone call in mind. It may be impossible to talk to that person with the prestigious title, but you can often contact someone else who can help you achieve the goal of your call.

In most telephone conversations, both parties have a good idea of "what's in it for me" even if it is never stated. The salesperson, for example, wants your order; you want the product. You want the product fixed; the customer service department wants a satisfied customer who will buy again.

Salespeople are trained to think, not about selling a product to a customer, but about the product's benefits. They know they don't sell drill bits, they sell holes. When you are trying to reach someone by telephone, you should know what *benefits* your conversation will have for the person you are calling. You may never have to mention the benefit, but if you know what it is, you can use it to persuade a secretary, an assistant, or a supervisor to let you speak to that person.

In some cases, knowing the benefit helps you choose the course of action. Are you getting satisfaction from the customer service department? If not, call your salesperson. The benefits may be hazy to a front-line customer service person who is just trying to get through a shift, but your salesperson knows future commission checks are on the line.

Do not overlook altruism. Most people like to help others. Be sure to let the person you are calling know if your conversation will help you. Of course, this approach loses its effectiveness quickly. Most people will be glad to help you a few times or do a small favor. But if you ask too often, people begin to expect something in return.

THE SCREENER

When most people talk about someone being difficult to get in touch with, they usually mean that the person has a secretary or other assistant that most callers can't get past. Someone who answers a business person's telephone with the goal of letting important calls in and keeping unimportant or misdirected calls out is called a screener.

Most people think their goal, when trying to reach a VIP with a screener, is to blow past the screener to get to the VIP. That is their first mistake.

A screener, no matter what his title is, is a gatekeeper. A screener controls access to the inner sanctum, but he also does so much more. When trying to reach someone by telephone, your first ally must be the screener. Learn the screener's name and take the time to say hello when you call. You never know when it will be helpful to have that ally in the office.

A screener is in the position to put your message on top of a pile, remind the boss to call you, or report on what a jerk you are. Many people recognize how valuable their own secretaries and assistants are, but some still treat other people's secretaries and assistants as barriers to getting through.

Screeners are also valuable sources of information. They may be able to tell you when you can expect your call to be returned or other information about the company. Let's say that you are looking for a job and are cold-calling companies. The company receptionist may be able to tell you

◆ if there are any job openings at the company;

◆ if the company is busy and growing or laying people off;

◆ if the company employs someone with the responsibilities or a job title similar to what you are looking for;

◆ the name of that person's supervisor.

When you reach the supervisor's secretary, you can ask

◆ if the department is planning to expand;

◆ what specific qualifications the supervisor is looking for in a candidate for the open position;

◆ the best time to reach the supervisor.

By using screeners as allies and sources of information, you have taken the chill out of your cold-call.

Screeners can also give you information about how calls like yours are usually handled. Because few people ask for this information, you can give yourself a leg up on the competition by knowing the rules before you begin, whether you are selling something, looking for a job, or wanting to file a complaint.

Some companies have a battalion of secretaries or executive assistants screening calls. When calling such a company, ask for the same screener you spoke with last time. If you have built rapport with this person, you won't have to start from scratch. Plus, people in general, and in particular people with vital but overlooked jobs, like to be remembered and noticed. By asking for your favorite screener by name, you've made another positive impression.

Even though screeners are an everyday part of business life, few people think about screeners at home. If you call your business customers at home, it's important for you to consider at-home, unpaid screeners too.

Many of the tactics for dealing with a secretary also work for dealing with a spouse, roommate, or older child who answers the phone and "screens" calls for your intended party. At the least, you should give this residential screener a reason to pass on a sales call to a loved one who may have asked not to have to deal with any.

The key to working the screeners is to consider them as a part of your telephone call and a step toward reaching your goal. Don't save up your request, question, or message for the person you hope to contact. As long as the question or information is not confidential, give the screener a summary of why you are calling or what you hope to accomplish.

Sometimes you will find that the screener can help you reach your goal without speaking to someone else at all—by giving you the date and time of the meeting you were calling to get, for example. Often the screener will just confirm that the person you are trying to reach is the best person to help you reach your goal. With that agreement, you have "sold" the screener that the VIP should take your call, and you can expect the screener to work for you, not against you, in making sure that you reach the VIP.

Sometimes the screener will tell you that there is a better person to speak to in order to achieve your goal. If you think the screener is misdirecting you, rephrase your goal and ask questions to determine whether the screener understands what you are looking for. If it turns out that there is a better person to speak to than the one you originally thought, you will have really benefitted by working with the screener. You will have saved time by not trying to reach the wrong person.

THE TECHNIQUE

When you have defined your goals, know the benefits of your call, and have the screener's agreement that you are trying to reach the right person, a few strategies will help you reach anyone by telephone. Circumstances can keep even two people who really want to speak together on the telephone from making a connection. This technique will help you avoid those circumstances.

There will always be people, however, who are rude or incompetent. No matter how good your telephone skills are, you cannot win against someone who doesn't follow the basic rules of business and society. This technique will help you get people who don't use the telephone effectively on the right track, but there is no magic wand to make rude people helpful or uncaring organizations more considerate of their customers.

Most of this process works equally well whether you are dealing with a live screener or a voice-mail system. We will discuss certain special tips for dealing with voice mail later in Chapter 8.

BE PERSISTENT

If the call is important to you and you cannot get through the first time, try again and again. How frequently you should call depends on how urgent the conversation is and if it is more important to you or the person you are calling. If you are calling to give someone information he requested, a single phone call is sufficient. Leave the information with a secretary if the person cannot answer your call or leave a message stating that you have the information.

If the call is more important to you, you can use some useful rules of thumb. If you must speak to someone by the end of the day, call back every few hours. Each time, leave a message explaining the urgency of your call. If you need to speak to someone within a few days or a week, call once a day. Ask what time of day is best to call or if there is one day when the person will be available, and call back at that day and time.

There is a big difference between being persistent and being a pest. The idea is to get across the urgency of your call and your willingness to make the call happen. If you try to harass people into calling you back, you may get the person to call, but she will probably be less responsive to what you have to say.

Let's say your personnel department is in charge of placing help wanted advertisements in the newspaper, and you have an opening in your department that needs to be filled immediately. You want to know if personnel has placed the ad. If the deadline for Sunday's paper is several days away, you may want to leave a message every day or so. If the deadline arrives and your call has still not been returned, leave a message every few hours and make it clear there is a deadline to be met. Keep in mind that the other party may be busy also. Don't cry wolf by marking a message urgent when the call can wait.

BE PATIENT

Don't be discouraged or feel insulted if your call is not promptly returned. If the person has been out of town, your message may be at the bottom of a huge stack. Many people return calls to people they know first, and then work their way through the unfamiliar names. When two or three message slips with your name on them pile up, your call may be bumped to the top of the stack.

If your call is not urgent, you should be willing to wait until the person has time to return it. Your reward for waiting will be a relaxed conversation and the full attention of the person. Remember to make the person you are calling aware of your deadlines. A relaxed conversation is worth nothing if it comes too late.

MAKE AN APPOINTMENT

One way to ensure that your conversation is both relaxed and prompt is to set up a time for the call ahead of time. It is a good idea to make an appointment or offer to make an appointment for any conversation you expect to last more than ten minutes. If you reach someone who sounds frantic, ask when to call back, even if the call will be a short one. The person will most likely appreciate how considerate you are of his time. In other cases, after you greet the person and explain briefly the purpose of your call, say, "I expect this to take twenty minutes. Do you have time to talk now?" If the person says no, ask what day and time you can call back.

Give the caller a specific time frame. Ask, "What time today would be better to call you?" or "What day this week is best for you?"

Don't let the fact that your "meeting" will take place by telephone lead you to making vague agreements about when you'll speak. If your prospect says, "Give me a call next Thursday afternoon," pin him down to a specific time.

With this vague statement your chances of catching the prospect at his desk and ready for your call are the same as if you were cold-calling. There are a number of ways to get a precise time and make it clear you consider it an appointment.

"What time on Thursday afternoon is best for you?" Or if Thursday is already jam-packed for you, offer choices of your openings.

Tell the person that you have noted the conversation on your calendar and confirm the exact date and time you will call. "I've got you on my calendar. I will give you a call on Thursday, the twenty-fifth at three o'clock on the dot." When he agrees, you've got yourself an appointment.

Treat a telephone appointment as you would any another appointment or meeting. Making an appointment also allows the person you are calling to treat the conversation like a meeting. The person has the opportunity to close the door, ask the secretary to hold calls, and have the materials you need on hand. Take advantage of the time you have to prepare and do the same thing. Making a telephone appointment gives you the advantage of talking to someone who has set aside a block of time to speak with you, but it can also make demands on your time.

When you make an appointment, make sure the person you are calling knows it is for a telephone meeting. Few people bother to make appointments for telephone calls, so occasionally there will be some confusion. Listen for the sigh of relief when you remind them that you want fifteen minutes of their time on the telephone, not in person.

BE FLEXIBLE

If you are trying to speak with someone who is very busy and you ask to make an appointment, the person may ask to make it before or after regular business hours. If the conversation will benefit you more than it will benefit the person you are calling, it is in your best interest to accommodate this request. In fact, if you want to do an end run around a call-screening system, try calling early in the morning, after business hours, or during lunch. Many busy executives answer their own telephone during these times, when their secretaries are at lunch or not at work.

You should also be flexible about which person you call. The one you call first may be able to refer you to someone else who can better help you or ask an assistant or staff member to handle your call. It is easy to forget the ultimate goal of your conversation when you are in hot pursuit. Don't lose focus. You should be willing to speak to anyone who can help you.

LEAVING A MESSAGE

When the call is very important to you and is not important or is even annoying for the person you are calling (such as a sales call), conventional wisdom says don't leave a message on voice mail or with an assistant. The idea is that, if the person calls you back, you may not be prepared for the call (such as when you are making a lot of cold-calls). Also, because the person will almost never call you back, leaving a message is just a waste of time.

There is a problem. When you reach a live screener and refuse to leave a message, the screener will automatically assume that you are a salesperson who does not have much confidence in her product or service. The screener may also think you are being uncooperative by refusing to leave a message as he just asked you to.

Instead of saying "no" and then asking when to call back, agree to leave a message. Then pause slightly and ask when the person you are trying to reach is expected to be available.

Agreeing to leave a message is more polite, lets the screener do his job, and is more likely to get the screener on your side. When you have the information, you can just say that you will call back then. If you are not making dozens of cold-calls, leave a message anyway *and* call back. If for some strange reason they actually return your call, you are one step ahead. If not, at least your name is familiar when you try again.

TIMING

Everyone is on a schedule of some sort, but some people are more aware of it than others. You may wake up every morning promptly at 7 A.M. and eat dinner every night at 6 P.M. At work it may seem like you just deal with things as they come up, but tracking your telephone calls, as discussed in Chapter 2, will probably reveal a pattern to your days that you may not have been aware of before.

The person you are trying to reach has a schedule too. And like you, she may not be aware of it. When the screener can't give you a good time to reach someone or when the person's voice-mail message gives no clue when is the best time to call, you may have to do a little detective work of your own.

When you are having difficulty reaching someone by telephone, consider that you may be trying to reach the person on your schedule, not theirs. Do you call every morning at 9 A.M. because you like to get your telephone calls out of the way? Perhaps the person you are trying to reach is not in the office that early. Vary your calling schedule. If you tried to reach the person in the morning on Tuesday, try late in the afternoon on Wednesday.

If you have reached this person before, or if she has called you, note the times the two of you have successfully made contact. In the future, consider this the best time to reach that person. Keep track of the time of day of each successful call in the same place you keep that person's telephone number. When you need to reach that person again, you will be able to select the most likely time to reach her.

BE APPRECIATIVE

We should all say thank you and show our appreciation for the help we get, but few of us do. Was a customer service representative particularly helpful? Call his boss and say so. Was your conversation with the southwestern regional sales director just what you needed to make your presentation a killer? Write her a thank-you note. Even just saying thank you at the end of the conversation paves the way for future successful conversations. If you are the one who shows appreciation, your calls will be returned promptly in the future.

WHEN YOUR CALLS ARE NOT RETURNED

Calls are often not returned. You left a message, but your call has not been returned, and you don't know why. The first step is to lay out the goal of your conversation, the benefits for the person you are calling, your deadline, and the consequences if the person does not return your call.

This is not the time for threats. You will be resented or, worse, sound silly. But if, for instance, your supplier does not understand that you will go to someone else for your order if you do not hear from him by 4 P.M., by all means spell it out. Leave this last-ditch message on voice mail or with a secretary or fax a note (ask the secretary or receptionist for the fax number).

If this doesn't work, you have a few options.

TALK TO THE BOSS

See if someone else can answer your question or if the company is simply not interested in what you have to say. Many managers hate to be bothered, so they will quickly direct you to the person who can help you. After they have done that, you have the extra leverage of having been referred by the boss. A secretary or assistant can also help you find someone else to talk to, but these people's names rarely open doors—unless they happen to be the boss's secretary or assistant.

WRITE A LETTER
Writing is a slow method, but sometimes letters get through when phone messages get lost. If your message is urgent, send the letter by fax.

MAKE A DRAMATIC STATEMENT
Send a letter or a telegram explaining the urgency of your message, or deliver flowers or balloons with your message attached. Just the right dramatic statement is magic, but don't overdo it. It is easy to

get dramatic in the heat of the moment. Before you make your dramatic statement, ask yourself how it will reflect on you and your company. Will it seem unprofessional or goofy? Will you come across as hysterical? Is it worth it?

HAVE A BACKUP OR A "BACK DOOR"

Do not tie yourself to one supplier or prospect. If you run into trouble, the easiest thing to do is move on to the next call. Sometimes simple inefficiency or bad business practices are keeping your calls from being returned. You must decide if you still want to do business with that company. Is there someplace else to get the information? Is there someone else at the company who can help you? Keep your ultimate goal in mind and try not to get sidetracked by the pursuit of a single person.

Let's say you want to buy a photocopier. You wonder if it needs to be on its own electrical circuit. The salesperson doesn't know, but she says she will give you a call. A few days pass, and you haven't received a call. You call the salesperson, and she says that the technical people haven't called her either. Is there someone else in the company who can help you? You may find out that the service manager can answer your question. Is there another source for this information? The manufacturer? A product brochure? If no one at this company can answer your question, or if they take a long time to reply, you may consider buying a copier from another company that will give you better service.

The key is not fixating on the call from the salesperson (or the technical people she is trying to reach). Focus on your goal: the information you need.

TAKE A STEP BACK

It can be very frustrating when you cannot reach someone by telephone. If this happens, it is best to take a step back and try to be objective.

Do you have a clear goal? Is the person you are trying to reach the best person to help you reach that goal? Have you asked that person's secretary or assistant if there is someone else who can help you? Have you explained to the person how he can benefit from your call?

Sometimes it is best to try another approach. The person may not be getting your messages or just may not respond well by telephone. Change your strategy. Send a message by letter, fax, or e-mail. Call at another time of day (when a busy executive may answer her own calls). Find another contact at the company.

VIPs may take a little longer—they require more motivation to return your calls—but a person is only as important as he is to you and your goals. Be persistent, patient, and accommodating, and you will increase your chances of reaching your VIP.

Chapter 6

Selling by Telephone:

More Effective Techniques from the Pros

"One of the best ways to persuade others is with your ears—by listening to them."

—Dean Rusk

The art of selling over the telephone is no mere skill—it is an industry in itself. This industry is often called telemarketing, but if you think that just means the untrained people who try to sell you magazine subscriptions while you are trying to eat dinner, you have just been scratching the surface of this wide-ranging industry.

Everything from orders for stocks and bonds costing millions of dollars to expensive industrial equipment to, well, discounted magazine subscriptions are sold over the telephone every day. You could fill an entire library with the books that have been written to guide people who sell by telephone for a living.

But what if your job title doesn't include the word *sales*? Even if your profession is personnel, accounting, or purchasing, you should know the basic techniques of selling over the telephone. Whether you need to convince a department that your recruitment plan is the best one, persuade your auditors that your internal controls are adequate, or set up a meeting with a client, you are selling over the telephone. Even non-salespeople do a lot of "selling" by phone.

Even though you are using telephone sales techniques for the more persuasive aspects of your job, make sure your staff understands the basics of sales too. Everyone who answers the telephone in your company is in sales. Helping the sales process can be as easy as knowing how to transfer a misdirected sales call to the proper person in the sales department. Or it may be as sophisticated as recognizing that someone who called for another purpose is a good sales lead for your product or service.

In both cases, knowledge is the key. You should train everyone who deals with your customers—from the accounting department to the shipping department—to recognize buying signals and to pass leads on to your sales force.

At minimum, make sure that everyone who might answer the phone in your company knows that, when a caller asks, "How can I buy...?" the answer "I don't know" is unacceptable. Give everyone the proper extension or telephone number in your sales department and make sure they know how to transfer the call. Or, instruct your staff to take the name and telephone number of any caller whose question they can't answer and pass the message to you.

If your company doesn't do this already, you will be surprised how many sales leads get lost because staffers don't know what to do with them. To make your sales lead program even more effective, consider offering a bonus to the person or group who uncovers a lead that leads to a sale.

CONSULTIVE SELLING

The world of sales is full of gimmicks. There is the "Ben Franklin close," various "probe" techniques, and the idea that a sale can be pulled together with a sure-fire "clincher."

After years of experience with these kinds of old-fashioned, hard-sell sales techniques, you may think telephone selling requires a silky voice, a well-rehearsed sales pitch, and a snappy answer for every objection. Actually, it requires none of these things. Skilled salespeople know that they are in the business of helping people. The technique they use is called *consultive selling*.

Consultive selling puts an emphasis on what the customer needs and wants. It involves listening more than talking; objections are addressed, not overcome. It focuses on questions. The seller asks a series of questions to find out if and how the seller's product, service, or idea will help the prospect. The questions are probing and open-ended. The salesperson looks for needs and desires that are not being met or that can be met more fully. For most of the process, the salesperson just listens.

If you are not naturally a salesperson, the consultive technique will make selling easier for you. It feels more like helping a customer than trying to talk a customer into doing something she doesn't want to do.

If you are a natural salesperson and have no trouble gaining people's confidence and then getting them to do what you want, you may think that using the consultive sales approach is not worth the time and effort. But consider this: unless your "sale" satisfies your customer, you won't be able to "sell" to them again.

Think of your sales presentation (even if it is just the presentation of an idea) as a Christmas gift. Think of your prospect or customer as a new staffer you have been asked to buy a Christmas gift for. You wouldn't run out and buy something without asking a lot of questions about that person first. How else will you know if your gift will fit the staffer's personality? In the same way, your sales presentation must fit your prospect if you are to make a sale that will lead to a long and happy relationship with your new customer.

PLANNING AHEAD

Consultive selling begins before you even pick up the telephone. According to Art Sobczak, president of Business By Phone, an Omaha, Nebraska-based telephone sales consulting and publishing firm, and publisher of the *Telephone Selling Report*, you should do these four things before making any persuasive call:

1. Write down specifically what you need to accomplish in this phone call. What do you want the person you are calling to do at the end of your conversation? What do you want to be doing?

2. Find out as much as possible about the person you are going to call.

3. Plan exactly what you are going to say in the first fifteen to twenty seconds of the phone call.

4. Prepare your questions.

When deciding what to say in the first few seconds of your call, plan to use this time to tell the person you are calling why he should be interested in your call. The person must know the benefit of staying on the telephone with you. In those first few seconds, you must explain

◆ who you are,

◆ why you are calling,

◆ what the benefits of the call are for the other party, and

◆ why he should spend time with you and answer your questions.

At the beginning of the call, become acquainted with the person you are calling; do not present a sales pitch. "Too many people give their presentation and their close before they know anything about the person they are selling to," says Sobczak. "You sell more by asking questions than by making statements."

Because questions, not a sales pitch, are the focus of consultive selling, carefully prepare your list of questions. Keep in mind that you are not calling to talk. Your objective is to listen. What do you need to know to persuade the person you are calling to take the course of action you want him to take? Do not limit yourself to practical matters. Hopes, dreams, and desires are powerful persuaders. When you have completed your precall planning, you are already ahead of most other people.

CHOOSING THE RIGHT PERSON

If you are trying to sell to people with a particular job title, such as the personnel director, do not simply ask to speak to the personnel director when you reach a company. Ask for the name of the person who holds that position, then ask to be transferred.

If a secretary answers the phone, take advantage of the opportunity to learn more about the person you are trying to reach. Ask the secretary what the boss is looking for in your product or service, or ask a question that gives you a better idea of what the person is like. Sobczak has found that a phrase like this works well: "I would like to speak to Ms. Johnson, but first can you tell me..."

ASKING QUESTIONS

When you reach your party, remember that you have approximately fifteen to twenty seconds to explain who you are and why the party you are calling should be interested in your call. When you have the person's attention, begin asking questions. "The only way to sell is by asking questions," says Sobczak. "Find out if there is a need, an interest, or an urgency. Find out if this person can make the decision and has the budget needed to buy your product or implement your idea."

Ask amplifying questions as well: "Please explain that." "Can you give me a specific example?" "Why do you follow that particular procedure?" "How did you reach that figure?" Sometimes a simple answer is not what it appears to be. Dig deeper. Find out what the person is really saying. If you settle for the pat answer, you will be hampered later on when you try to use the information you have gathered.

There are *recognized* and *unrecognized* needs. If you are lucky, your prospect will know what she needs. But if she doesn't recognize her company's needs, you must help her. You can do this by asking more questions or making statements that make her company's needs more apparent to her.

When you are digging for information, ask your question in a way that assumes a thorough answer, not just a yes or no. Don't ask "Do you have any questions?" Ask "What questions do you have?"

This is called an *open question,* and it is the preferred way of asking questions during a sales interview—or any other interview. There are times, however, when you will benefit by asking a yes or no question, also known as a *closed-ended question*:

◆ When you know the other person is in a hurry.

◆ When you already have a good relationship with the other person and you don't need the small talk to build rapport.

◆ When you are looking for facts and figures.

◆ When you use them to add variety to your interviewing.

Even when you make your presentation, you can be more effective by asking questions instead of making statements. It is a way to make your customer feel smart. Instead of making a statement or telling your customer what to do, think of a question that would help your prospect reach the same conclusion. For example, instead of saying, "Using our product will save you two hours each day," try saying, "What would happen if you could print twice as much before restocking the paper tray?"

This technique takes a little practice, so try it in less important situations first. It is easy to talk down to your prospect using this technique. The idea is to let your prospect use her own brains to reach the conclusion. The secret to success is all in your tone of voice.

MAKING THE PRESENTATION

The next step, the actual presentation, is easy if you have spent time getting to know your prospect. Because you already know about her, you can focus on the benefits and features that will fill her company's needs. Your presentation can be brief. If your prospect is interested in the bottom line, tell her how your proposed work schedule will save money. If she is interested in safety, show how it will reduce job-related injuries. If you did not know your prospect you would have to give her every detail, hoping to hit on one or two that appealed to her. Because you have already analyzed what appeals to her, you can deliver just the meat of the presentation.

"When I give a seminar, this is the shortest part of my discussion," says Sobczak. "You have found out their wants, needs, and desires. There has to be one specific item you can address." Because you know these things, tailor your presentation to address what you have discovered.

What happens when your prospect gives you a time limit? Often people who receive many sales calls do this to try to save themselves from wasting time with inappropriate sales pitches.

If you follow all the steps we've discussed so far, you will probably never be put under this kind of pressure. You've already given your prospect a reason to spend time with you by mentioning a benefit in your opening statement. You probably won't be cut off while asking questions, because few people think to make a time limit when they are the ones talking.

But let's say you are ready to make your presentation, perhaps after questioning the prospect in a previous call, and your prospect gives you two minutes.

One trick is not to rush. Know that you can't cram your presentation into such a small time frame. Instead, focus on a key benefit that you know appeals to your prospect. Once the prospect is involved in your conversation, ask for a time check. Ask if you should you keep the conversation going or call back another time.

When presenting to a senior executive, keep it short even if you are not given a time limit. Executives tend to be "big picture" people who are bored by a lot of detail. Aim for a brief package of information and have the details to back it up if the executive asks for more.

When making your presentation you will know what your prospect's needs and motivations are, but don't take the extra step of making all your prospect's decisions for him. If he mentions being on a tight budget, suggest your lower-priced product or service, but by all means, mention the more expensive option. Your prospect may be so impressed by the benefits of the more expensive option that money outside the budget can be found for that alternative. Even better, if you can show how the more expensive alternative will actually save money in the long run, you may make the sale.

When making a presentation over the telephone, be aware of all your prospect's five senses. It's much easier to sell something that your prospect can see, hear, touch, taste, smell, and see (assuming that it looks and smells good!). Because the prospect can't do this over the telephone, use words to describe the product or service in as many senses as possible.

If you are selling something over the phone, such as a food or beverage, that people usually want to taste or see before they buy, offer a guarantee. The quality of your guarantee (such as money back if they are not happy) can assure a prospect about buying something in a new way.

CLOSING THE SALE

Even though you are avoiding the hard sell, you must remember to *close*—to ask for the sale or agreement with your proposal. Every Girl Scout knows she must ask, "Would you like to buy some cookies?" It is hard to believe that adults—even professional salespeople—forget or avoid asking for an agreement. Actually, it is very common.

Many salespeople find themselves with a long list of prospects to call back and few sales. This is the sign of a poor closer or a salesperson who is afraid to ask for an agreement.

After getting so involved with your prospect, you may find it awkward to bluntly ask him to do what you want. Sobczak recommends saying, "Based on what you've already told me, it sounds as if you already have made up your mind."

Here are some other ways Sobczak suggests for asking your prospect for a commitment:

◆ Why don't I ship you one?

◆ So you will have those inventory figures prepared by the next time we speak, is that right?

◆ Would you like to buy it?

◆ Are you comfortable taking this to the boss with your recommendation that you go with it?

◆ The next time you need supplies, would you buy them from me?

◆ Is this the program that you'd personally like to invest in?

◆ Shall we get started?

◆ If you do decide to change vendors before my next call, will you call me?

If a decision cannot be made immediately, make sure you both know what has to be done next. Every persuasive call should end with both parties taking some action. Have the person send you something by mail—such as a union contract specifying certain work hours, in the case of the work schedule change. If the person you spoke to must get someone else's approval to proceed, make sure she is sold first. The prospect is now your salesperson. Ambivalence on the part of this person won't do your cause much good. Your prospects should know what you will be doing next. Will you mail them further information? Get back to them with the answer to a question?

ANSWERING OBJECTIONS

Chances are your prospect will not immediately say "yes" when you close. Instead he may have objections. "The best way to answer an objection is to ask more questions, not to fire off a prepared response," says Sobczak.

Luckily, most people hate to say no. Unfortunately, most people will not be specific about their reasons for not agreeing with you.

Respond to objections with "Let's talk about that." For example, a colleague may say he won't back your proposal because of the financial impact on the company. What she may mean is that she is afraid your proposal will postpone an expansion of her department. If you fire back a retort explaining the financing of your proposal in general terms, you won't have answered her real objection.

"Talking through objections is a painless way to pull your chair over to the other side of the desk," says Sobczak. "Don't try to overcome objections; instead, answer them. Overcoming an objection implies a winner and a loser—and you don't want that."

This is the point in the sales process where the depth of your knowledge is tested. Some objections are really requests for more information. If you don't know more about your product or service than your prospect does, you won't be able to answer these objections.

Other objections are more confrontational. They may sound as though the prospect is doubting what you said. Instead of trying to counter these objections, try, as Sobczak said, to pull your chair over to the other side of the desk. Ask yourself under what circumstances that view would be true. Ask yourself what would cause someone to say that.

When you have done this, you will be in a better frame of mind to discuss your prospect's objection and deal with it in a friendly, conversational way.

THE TRIANGLE APPROACH

Think of persuading or selling as a triangle with the point at the bottom. The width of the triangle is the amount of time you spend on each stage. You need to spend a lot of time before you even make the call. You must know what you need to accomplish and something about the person you are speaking with. You need to plan what you will say in the first few seconds and you must prepare questions to find out more about the person and his needs.

When you ask the questions, you primarily will be listening. The question-and-answer stage can take a long time. Once your questions are answered satisfactorily, you can make your presentation: explain to the person why he should support your idea or buy your product. This statement can be brief. Focus on the points you know will interest your prospect or co-worker.

And don't forget the brief phrase in which you ask for agreement on the sale. "Will you back me in the meeting?" or "Will you buy the product?" This phrase is the point of the triangle, and the point of your call.

If the person says "no," ask why he doesn't agree with you. (Don't mistake no answer for a "no.") Don't overcome the person's objections, answer them. Say "Let's talk about that" to get the person to elaborate on his response. Again, you are listening more than talking. You are back at the question-and-answer stage.

KEEPING IN TOUCH

If your first pass through the selling process doesn't result in a "sale," most experts recommend keeping in touch with your prospect until conditions change in favor of making a sale. The experts also suggest keeping past customers on your list of prospects. These former customers are actually one of your best sources for future customers.

Too often though, salespeople keep in touch with their inactive accounts by calling and asking, "Why haven't you bought?" This is an awkward question for several reasons. (You may be their biggest supplier.)

A better idea is the thank-you approach. Call the customer or prospect and thank her for her past business. Then tell her about a new product or service. If your customer has been "inactive" because she was unhappy with your company, you will certainly hear about it.

When your relationship with your prospect or customer is more persuasive than sales-oriented, keeping in touch can be more subtle and more social. Some ideas for keeping in touch include sending

◆ a birthday or holiday card,

◆ articles of interest,

◆ articles about your company and other publicity, or

◆ ideas relating to a project you have discussed.

Another trap you can fall into with either type of keeping-in-touch call is simply asking, "How are you?" with no other point to the call. You should make sure each call, even a keeping-in-touch call, has value for the other party. So instead of calling every month, call with good news, information you know will help them, an idea to help their business, or details on a special you are running. Each call should have a reason.

Keep in mind that the whole point of these keeping-in-touch calls is to be available when a change in your favor occurs. To find out when this happens, you have to ask. But don't just ask, "What's new?" Your prospect will reflexively answer, "Not much, what's new with you?" That's not what you are after.

Instead, ask "What has changed in your sales department since the last time we spoke in April?"

WHEN TO LET GO

If all this sounds time-consuming, maybe even too time-consuming to be practical, you are partly right. If you try to keep in touch with every prospect you ever come in contact with, much of your time will be wasted. The idea is to keep in touch with those prospects whose relationship can benefit you and to let the others go.

Because chasing after a prospect who will never buy your product or service or support your idea is a big waste of time, especially if you are going to hear a "no," it is best to hear it as early as possible. Don't be afraid of hearing "no." Make it easy for your prospects to tell you no. If you never cross people off your list of prospects, you will always have a long list, but you will probably not have the time to make any sales.

One way to hear "no" in a timely way is to make sure something happens during every sales call you make or get. Have your prospect do something that moves them toward your ultimate goal. If they aren't willing to do it, you are probably wasting your time. Consider any decision, even a "no," progress.

SCRIPTS

In some companies, fairly untrained telephone personnel read scripts when making a sales call instead of going through the process just described. There is certainly nothing wrong with this technique, especially if the sales campaign requires reaching many people in a short amount of time and the product or service being sold is very simple for everyone to understand.

These sales scripts are usually written by professionals with years of experience selling by telephone. These experts can be hired on a free-lance basis. If you must write a telephone sales script yourself, build the techniques discussed here into your script.

Prepare a benefit-rich opening statement for your sales reps to read. By law, your reps must tell your prospects the name of your company, and it is a good idea to have the reps introduce themselves too. Give the reps a list of questions to ask that will reveal the needs and motivations of the people they call. You will probably find that all your prospects have just a few basic needs or motivations. Prepare a presentation tailored to each of these needs.

Reading a script and making it sound real is a rare skill. Many telemarketing companies like to hire actors to make these types of scripted calls. One of the basic things these actors bring to the technique is a nice, slow pace. The right pace for reading a sales script feels a little too slow to the person who is speaking it. Remember to have the reps speak clearly, especially when saying their names and the names of your company.

PRACTICE, PRACTICE, PRACTICE

More than any other type of telephone call, making an effective sales call requires practice. But just making many sales calls isn't effective practice. First, tape record your sales calls. Listen to them later, and make sure you hit all the steps in the sales process. Did you give a benefit to start? Were you a good listener? Did you tailor your presentation to your prospect's needs? How did your voice sound?

"There are grizzled, veteran salespeople who have placed thousands of calls, but have no real experience to speak of," says Sobczak. That is because they don't review their calls or reflect on what they have done.

At the end of every sales call, he says, you must ask yourself:

◆ What did I like about this call?

◆ What would I have done differently on this call?

Do you think you don't have time to do this after every sales call? You can't afford not to.

When you use a consultive selling approach, both sides win. Even if you do not persuade your co-worker to back you in this case, you begin a relationship and sow the seeds for future agreements. If the elements needed for both sides to be satisfied do not exist now, things may come together down the road. If you do not change anyone's mind on your first call, do not give up.

A study conducted by the marketing department at the University of Notre Dame showed that the average telephone sale was made after five attempts to close the sale. Yet many telephone sellers give up long before that. When you use professional selling techniques that benefit the person you are calling as much as they benefit you, those phone calls are easier to make and more likely to end in success.

Chapter 7

Customer Service by Telephone:

The Art of Keeping Customers

"Give the customer what she wants!"

—Marshall Field

There are many parallels between offering customer service by telephone and selling by telephone. Both are industries in themselves, with newsletters, articles, trade show seminars, and consulting services dedicated to teaching practitioners the finer points of the activity. Both have entire departments devoted to them in large corporations. Both are much simpler to perform face to face.

The sales department may be selling now, but customer service is selling for the future. The idea behind customer service is future sales. The goal of customer service is to have existing customers continue to do business with your company, or even increase the amount of business they do if possible. Another goal is to increase company sales by word of mouth from satisfied customers. Keep these two goals in mind when you deal with customers over the telephone.

Just as you probably have to sell by telephone for your job even if your job title doesn't include the word *sales*, you will almost certainly have to offer customer service over the phone even if your job couldn't be farther from your company's customers. Your department may serve one or more types of customers. You may be in direct contact with the people who buy your company's products or services. In this case, how you interact with these customers over the telephone can be the difference between a faithful, life-long customer, and one who never buys from your company again and bad-mouths it at every opportunity.

You may only deal with other employees of your company, but these employees are still "customers" of your department. If they are not happy with the service you provide, you may find no allies when your company decides to outsource your department's function or makes painful cuts to your budget. Good customer service starts with how employees treat each other. By treating your internal customers well, the whole company is able to offer better service to external customers.

The term *customer service* includes most interactions with customers, whether those customers are internal or external. Answering questions, providing information, and especially solving problems are all customer service functions.

When we think of customer service we usually think of a face-to-face interaction. For example, the clerk in a department store who handles the exchange of your Christmas gift may come to mind. Customer service over the telephone follows all the same principles of face-to-face customer service, except both parties are limited to using only their voices over the telephone to give and receive information.

When you return a gift in a department store, the clerk can walk you over to another register. Simply transferring a telephone call to the correct employee does not convey the same sense of caring. (Stay on the line and summarize the caller's problem for the person you are transferring the call to.) In person you can see if a customer's face turns red. You can calm the customer with a smile. Over the telephone, you need to listen for signs of emotion and express yourself with words as well as actions.

Using good call-handling skills is the first step toward effective customer service over the telephone. How is a caller greeted? Everyone who answers a telephone in your company should be courteous and willing to help. Putting a caller on hold before she can say a word is not courteous. Keeping a caller on hold for a long time can also erode customer relations.

Try this experiment. Set a timer for one minute. Close your eyes and sit still until the timer rings. Could you get through the entire minute without peeking at the timer? When callers are on hold, they are in the dark—just as you are sitting with your eyes closed. Sure, there may be music on hold to help pass the customers' time, but they really want to talk to someone. That's why they called. While you are busy handling other calls or looking for information, they are sitting in the dark.

If you must put callers on hold for more than a few seconds, let them know how long you expect to put them on hold and ask for their permission. If you think you will be away longer than a minute, ask if you can call back.

You may think that your customers don't expect great customer service over the telephone. Your company may not compete directly with companies known for their excellent service such as Federal Express or L. L. Bean, so you may think that you can get away with less. But those companies have raised the stakes for everyone. Your customers probably deal with a company that is offering excellent customer service over the telephone, and they expect no less from you.

HELP YOUR CO-WORKERS

Your department is used to answering the just plain stupid phone calls you get with patience, knowledge, and diplomacy. These are the calls that confuse your company with another or that completely misinterpret what your company sells or provides. But what happens when those calls go to another department?

Come up with a very brief script to cover the top two or three stupid questions your department receives. (They always seem to be the same ones, don't they?) The script should include the information in the most precise way possible and directions on what to do with the call. (Should they all go to sales? Customer service? Be directed to the proper company?) Your co-workers will thank you.

LISTENING SKILLS

Besides good call-handling skills, the next most important skill in telephone customer service is listening. Interrupting, planning what you are going to say next while the other person is talking, and saying something that has no relation to what the person just said are all examples of poor listening.

A good listener puts aside other work while on the telephone. Don't file, don't look up telephone numbers, don't consult your calendar, don't write a memo. Listening takes all your attention, so don't give your customer less than your whole attention.

You don't have to sit at your desk with your hands folded while listening, though. In fact, it is a good idea to take notes. You should have paper and a pen near your telephone anyway. While your customer is talking, take notes on what he is saying. This will not only give you a record of your conversation, but it may also stop you from interrupting because you are afraid of forgetting an important point. With the highlights of the customer's conversation in front of you, you will remember what you wanted to say.

Another good listening skill is often called *active listening*. This is rephrasing what customers say in your own words after they finish speaking. Note that this is not merely repeating what the customer says. It is easy to repeat something without ever understanding what is said. Active listening guarantees that what the customer said actually gets processed by your brain. You have to understand what is said before you can put it into your own words.

For example, if the customer says, "When I turn the ignition key, nothing happens." By active listening, you might say, "So your car won't start."(At this point you are just trying to rephrase what the customer says. Later we'll talk more about digging deeper into customer problems using a similar technique.)

HOW TO GET PEOPLE TALKING

Sometimes the problem isn't listening while there are distractions all around you, but rather getting the customer to talk in the first place. The key to getting people to talk is asking questions. Of course you must ask the right question at the right time. Here are some suggestions:

◆ If your customer pauses after you ask a question, don't rush to answer it yourself. Imagine them thinking. Give them time to gather their thoughts and then respond.

◆ Don't rush in after you have asked a question either. Let a few seconds of silence tick by. The customer may not be finished or may think of something new, and valuable to you, in those few seconds.

◆ Make sure it is a good time to talk. You can often hear in someone's voice if they are busy or tired. If not, just ask if this is a good time to talk or if there is a better time.

◆ If you think your customer's mood is related to the subject of your telephone call, mention it and ask for more information.

◆ Ask concrete questions. Most people live in the present and don't like theorizing. (Consultants and "experts" are different. They build cloud castles for a living.) Most people need to be asked questions that draw directly on their experiences. "Has a delay in thumbtack delivery ever caused problems for your company?" is better than "Could poor service cause a problem?"

◆ If you have spoken with the customer before, get her talking by following up on what you spoke about last time.

◆ Talk a little (very little) about yourself or your company to get the ball rolling.

◆ To get past the obvious, ask for multiples. Ask, "What's the most important factor in your thumbtack purchases?" and you will hear "price." Ask for the *three* most important factors and you'll have more to work with.

◆ Don't ask for the most or the least. There's a certain personality type that panics when asked to pick *just one*. Blunt their panic by asking for a few examples. Don't ask, "What's the biggest problem you've had with the thumbtacks you've purchased in the past?" (You can practically hear them thinking, "Was that the worst or was the other thing the worst?") Ask instead, "Can you tell me about a few of the problems you've had with thumbtacks?"

◆ Set the tone of the answer with the tone of your question. If you are an expert, questioning another expert, and want to cut to the chase, load your question with technical terms, insider knowledge and talk quickly. You will get a similar answer. (Of course, everyone had better be an expert, or this is disaster.) On the other hand, if you are not an expert, don't try to show off what little you do know by using technical terms. Ask your question in jargon-free language, use simple phrases, and don't rush the question.

◆ Ask what you have forgotten to ask. You'll fall flat with this one if you weren't thorough to begin with. But if you were probing and listened well, this could be a gold mine. You can ask this question only after a series of related questions. "What did I neglect to ask you about how your company uses thumbtacks that you think is important?" Sometimes they'll say, "Nothing." That's okay. Sometimes they will ramble. Listen for useful tidbits.

BE PROMPT

Even the best listening and questioning skills won't do any good if they come too late. Speed is an important element of customer service. Calls should be answered quickly. Messages should be returned promptly. Problems should be solved as soon as possible.

The telephone is immediate. When someone picks up the phone he expects things to happen quickly. If he is calling to complain, not receiving fast service can actually make the situation worse. While they are waiting on hold or waiting for their call to be returned, they are fuming. Soon your delay becomes as big a problem as the one that first prompted their call.

USING LONG DISTANCE

Don't be afraid to call a customer back long distance. National companies with 800 numbers are used to spending money on long distance phone calls to serve customers, but "local" companies need to lose their fear of long distance charges. The fact is, there is no such thing as a local company any more.

Any local business, from an insurance agent to a restaurant, occasionally gets calls from out-of-town customers. If you are afraid to spend a few dollars (at most) to make that call, then you will lose out on the reservation for the big business dinner, and the new resident will get her homeowner's policy elsewhere.

SPEAK YOUR CUSTOMER'S LANGUAGE

Every company and industry has its own vocabulary to describe departments, products, and procedures. But the burden is on you to speak your customers' language. Forcing them to learn your terms is not good service.

If your receptionist asks, "Would you like to speak to Reflections or Fine Assets?" you are confusing your customer. It's better to describe the options than to use company shorthand. "Are you interested in our line of fine china or our silver flatware?"

When you have been at your company a while, slang and specialized terms used in your company or industry start creeping into your everyday language. Using this jargon with customers is a no-no. First, customers are confused by expressions they don't understand. Second, using these terms gives customers a peek behind the wizard's curtain. You want their focus on the customer service stage, not on your office operations.

Another excellent tactic taught by top customer service trainers is to listen to special vocabulary or terms used by your customer and use them yourself. Done right, this practice gives you instant credibility and rapport. But it is very easy to do incorrectly. Too many business people use the unfamiliar terms in quotation marks. You can actually hear the quotation marks over the phone. "We offer the '24 by seven' tech support you require." The result is more mocking than rapport building.

Also, some people hesitate before using the unfamiliar term. Perhaps they are stumbling. Perhaps they wrongly believe that the prospect must notice their use of the term for it to be effective. This is a subtle, almost subliminal, tactic. If you are not confident you can use it well, don't use it at all.

A QUESTION OF UNDERSTANDING

You probably know that you should never ask a customer, "Are you stupid?" But asking "Do you understand?" or "Are you following me?" are nearly as insulting to your customer's intelligence. Because the burden is on you to communicate your points, phrase the question that way. "Did I explain that clearly enough?" "Did I go into enough detail on that?"

HANDLING IRATE CUSTOMERS

Most customer service is routine: handling requests for product information and routing a telephone call to the proper party. They are neutral interactions where neither party is showing much emotion of any kind. Offering excellent service during these calls is a challenge just because they are boring. But in a small percentage of calls sparks fly. An angry customer can set your pulse racing, making it even more difficult to offer excellent service while solving the problem.

An irate customer may call and yell. Or the customer may calmly tell you how horrible she thinks your product or service is. As hard as it is to listen to this, you should let the customer blow off some steam. If the customer is not abusive, just let her vent. Think of irate customers as volcanoes. It is dangerous to approach (interrupt) while they are erupting, but after the eruption is past, your work can begin.

When customers vent their anger without interruption, they may pause or they may apologize. If you try to interrupt before they are through, chances are they will just blow up again after you have finished talking. When the customer is through, bring them back down to earth by making appropriate sympathetic or empathetic comments. You don't have to take blame, agree, or even sympathize with everything the customer said. If there is only one small thing you can sympathize with, go with that. You can use your active listening to come up with a neutral statement that shows the customer you have listened and understood.

For example, you might say, "I can see why you would be upset after losing your luggage on vacation." This is just as appropriate if the lost luggage is entirely the customer's fault as if it is entirely your company's fault. The idea here is not to place blame—don't try to. The idea is to soothe the customer.

This is also the time to introduce yourself if you were not able to do so at the beginning of the conversation. An irate customer does not expect anyone to take responsibility. You don't have to take responsibility for causing the person's problem, but if you take responsibility for solving it, your customer will probably calm down considerably. Spell your name, give your title. Let the customer know who you are.

Another soothing tactic is a soft compliment. For example, you may compliment the customer for making the phone call. "It was wise of you to call me. It is my job to help customers find their luggage." The trick here is to find something you can say sincerely. Very few of us are good enough actors to give an insincere compliment. Customers can hear in your voice when you are offering a false compliment.

If tempers are still flaring after the customer has vented and you have made an attempt at soothing him, take a break. Offer to call the customer back, either in a few minutes or the next morning. Use the time to gather your own composure, review tactics, and perhaps confer with co-workers who have handled similar problems. Taking a break is also a good idea if the customer is being abusive or using bad language.

When the customer is calm, be sure to use active listening and probing questions to get to the root of the problem. Few people express themselves well when they are irate. Give your customer the chance to clarify the problem. Use your understanding of your company's products and services to find the problem behind the problem that the customer may not be aware of.

For example, the customer with the "lost" luggage may have expected his luggage to be waiting in the hotel lobby when it had already been brought to his hotel room. He may be searching the baggage carousel for a different flight, or his oversized luggage may have been brought to a special area.

Even if the customer made a simple mistake, don't make him feel stupid for doing so. Even if the customer has just been yelling at you, and possibly making you feel stupid, don't turn the tables. There is no such thing as retaliation in customer service.

If the fault lies more with your company than with the customer, or if what you can do for the customer is not as much as he would like you to do, you must use careful phrasing to present the solution in the most positive light. Don't say "I can't help you until you fill out a claim form." Say "I can help you as soon as you fill out a claim form." This takes a little practice, but it will bring you big rewards in customer service.

TAKING AN EXTRA STEP

It may seem hard to believe, especially in the thick of solving someone's problem, but it is possible to turn your company's customer service disaster into an incident that actually wins you a customer for life. First, make the customer better off than she was before the complaint. This means going one step beyond just apologizing for the problem.

Next, don't just solve the problem, do something extra. You are not doing the customer a favor by simply providing what you should have provided in the first place. To take advantage of the opportunity to win a customer for life, you must offer something in addition to the solution of the problem the customer called about.

Finally, don't close the books on a customer service transaction until you are sure the customer is satisfied. This may mean staying on the telephone until the customer understands exactly what steps she should take next. Or it may mean making a follow-up phone call after an item has been repaired or replaced to make sure everything is as expected.

If you believe the problem is solved, but the customer is still talking, consider that the customer may have other issues to discuss or may not understand what has happened. Or the customer, having found a kind soul to talk to, is just taking up your time. In any case, a simple "Have I answered all your questions?" should wrap up the conversation.

HANDLING STRESS

Customer service, especially solving customer problems, is a high-stress job. Even if you only handle customer complaints occasionally, you may find your pulse racing or your mouth dry when you hang up from the call. To preserve your health and to be in good condition to solve the next problem that comes your way, try these tactics:

◆ Take a deep breath. It's simple, but it really works.

◆ Talk to co-workers—not to complain about your job or bash the customer but just to assure yourself that this sort of thing happens sometimes and that you still have the sympathy of your peers.

◆ Try to see the humor in the situation. The biggest customer service nightmares become the funniest customer service stories— once the wounds have healed. Speed up the process by seeing the humor now.

◆ Put the incident in perspective.

◆ Try to learn something.

A LITTLE SYMPATHY

Soft compliments, sympathetic comments, understanding, and treating others as you would like to be treated are effective methods. Most customer service tactics involve putting yourself in your customer's place. Offering good customer service over the telephone is easier if you understand your customers. That's why companies that emphasize customer service encourage employees to use their products and services.

It's easier to empathize with an airline customer lost in the airport if you are a frequent flier yourself. The idea isn't to side with the customer against your company but to be able to offer sincere sympathy to the customer's situation. "I know, I often can't find the baggage carousels myself in big airports." And if you mostly deal with customers by telephone, having first-hand knowledge of their experiences can help you solve their problems better, when you can't see the environment they are in when they call.

If, when he hangs up the phone, your customer feels as though he not only solved a problem but made a friend at your company, you have thoroughly succeeded in your customer service mission. After all, when it's time to buy your company's product or service again, that customer will turn to you. Most people would rather do business with a friend.

Chapter 8

Using Voice Mail:

A Help or a Hindrance to Your Telephone Effectiveness?

"Perhaps the most important thing that has come out of my life is the discovery that if you prepare yourself . . . you will be able to grasp opportunity. . . . Without preparation you cannot do it."

—Eleanor Roosevelt

"I hate voice mail!" is a cry heard all over the business world—and beyond. Even the syndicated newspaper column "Dear Abby" dedicated several days to readers' gripes about voice mail (and one day to its defense). Interestingly, most of these readers' complaints were not about voice mail—the automated recording and playing of messages over telephone lines—but rather about automated attendants, which as we will see in Chapter 10, are something else entirely.

Voice mail functions just like your answering machine at home. When callers reach a voice-mail system, they hear a previously recorded greeting and then have the opportunity to leave a recorded message of their own. Many people strongly objected to answering machines when they first became popular, and there are still a few people out there who don't own one and refuse to leave a message on one. It may be those same people who so strongly object to voice mail. But this technology must be working for many businesses or it would not be so popular.

It is hard to justify hating voice mail as a technology. Like almost any other technology, it's not the device itself that causes strong feelings but how it is used by people who have a wide range of skill and awareness. Perhaps the most frustrating habit voice mail inspires among some users is "hiding" behind the technology. Hiding behind voice mail is when someone forwards her telephone to the voice-mail system even when she is available to take calls—and then does not return the messages left on the system.

This is exactly the same as throwing away all the pink while-you-were-out message slips handed to you by a secretary. The problem is not with the technology, which merely turned pieces of pink paper into electronic bits and bytes, but with the employee for poor business practices and with management for not training the employee and not making the employee accountable for returning telephone calls.

Although the technology that makes voice mail possible continues to evolve, the concepts behind using it effectively remain as true today as when the first primitive systems began taking messages nearly twenty years ago.

LEAVING VOICE-MAIL MESSAGES

Used correctly, voice mail is a valuable tool to enhance your personal effectiveness and your company's productivity. Even if your company does not have voice mail, you are sure to encounter this technology when calling other firms. If you follow the basic telephone principles discussed in Chapter 1 you will already be far ahead of most callers when you need to leave a voice-mail message.

When it comes to leaving voice-mail messages, your motto should be "be prepared." If you have planned the goals of your call before picking up the telephone, you won't be thrown off when you encounter voice mail.

Research done by the voice-mail industry shows that fifty percent of all phone calls are "one way." One person needs to deliver information to another. With voice mail you don't have to wait until the person calls you back—if you are prepared. When calling to deliver *one-way information*, be ready to leave a complete and coherent message on voice mail. The voice-mail system is secure enough for even confidential messages. Voice-mail systems require users to enter their mailbox address and password before they can retrieve their messages.

But, even though a voice-mail mailbox is more secure than a pink message slip, it is not totally secure. Telephone system hackers inside and outside the company you are calling have been known to crack mailbox passwords and listen to messages. You can be fairly confident that only the person you are calling will hear your message, but you certainly wouldn't want to leave any information that could be life-shattering or a security risk, such as sensitive medical information or the combination to the office safe.

For people who do business nationwide, voice mail has an added benefit in addition to the ability to leave detailed messages: you do not have to wait until office hours to "speak" to people outside your time zone. If you have a brainstorm at 6 P.M. in California, you can leave a message for someone in New York (even though it is 9 P.M. there) and know that it will be received first thing in the morning.

If you dread talking to a chatty business associate, voice mail can come to your rescue. Call to give information at a time when you are sure the verbose associate is not available to take your call. Leave your message on voice mail and avoid the other person's time-wasting ramble. This is also a good way to save time if you must make many short telephone calls to deliver information. Even if you love speaking with the people you need to call, the most basic social pleasantries will make your task drag on forever. Make these calls outside of normal business hours, and you can complete your task quickly.

Be very careful when making calls before or after normal business hours—especially if you get to work very early or work very late.

More people are working from home these days, so you should be sure you will reach a corporate voice-mail system or the person's answering machine before trying to leave a message at an off hour. Although accidently getting a home-worker out of bed at 3 A.M. makes a funny story later, it is not a good business practice.

If you are using the telephone effectively, you will yearn to leave a detailed message when you can't reach the person you are calling. Secretaries and other message takers usually don't have the time to write down your detailed messages, so leaving a voice-mail message is very helpful.

Most voice-mail systems let you record a message of any length. Even the ones that put a limit on the length of the message often give you a minute or more. That is long enough for even the most detailed message. Take advantage of it. It is not long enough to leave a rambling message filled with pauses though, so make your point quickly.

Voice mail excels at communicating complicated messages. How many times has this happened to you? You call the shipping department for information on the status of an order. The person you need to speak to is in a meeting, so the department secretary takes a message. Hours later your call is returned. The first question your shipping person asks is "What did you want?" And, of course, she will have to get back to you later for the ship date on that order.

Voice mail makes things much easier if both parties know what they are doing. Instead of just leaving a message to call you back, leave a message detailing the information the shipping department needs to track the order. You do not need to worry about giving too much detail. Most voice-mail systems let the recipient rewind and fast-forward messages much like a tape recorder. (Just remember to speak slowly and clearly—voice mail still cannot fix a garbled message.) With the detail you provide, the person should be able to return your call with an answer to your question, or mail you the brochure, catalog, or information you requested if you leave your address.

Encountering voice mail is probably most frustrating for salespeople. Don't despair when you reach voice mail when making a cold-call. Voice mail is a great selling opportunity if you can leave a thirty second "commercial." Keep the goals of the commercial simple: building name recognition, introducing benefits, and, just maybe, inspiring a call back.

STEP BY STEP

Getting someone's voice mail instead of the person live is a disappointment, but take advantage of the situation. Listen closely to how the person pronounces his name in the voice-mail greeting. Jot down the name with a phonetic spelling so you can pronounce it correctly the next time you call.

Also listen to the content of the message. Effective voice-mail users will tell you when to expect a return call and the name and extension of someone who can help you if your call is urgent. They will ask you for important information they need to answer your question. Sometimes the message will alert you to a change: a new telephone number, a change in job responsibility, or an extended leave. It is amazing how many people ignore the information in a recorded greeting. Listen carefully, and you may find a way to reach your goal sooner.

If the voice-mail greeting does not leave specific instructions about how to phrase your message, start by giving your name and your company's name and then your telephone number. If your call is cut off (which can happen for many reasons), at least your call can be returned. Plan to leave your telephone number at least twice during the message.

Even if the person you are calling has a voice-mail system that lets them rewind and replay messages, they will appreciate it if they can get your number down the first time they hear it. When leaving your name and number on voice mail, slow down! Use this test: jot each digit down on a piece of scrap paper after you say it. Then say the next digit. Before long the pacing will become habit.

And always leave your telephone number when you leave a voice-mail message—even if the person you are calling calls you frequently. One of the big advantages of voice mail is that users do not need to be in the office to retrieve their voice-mail messages. They do not even need to call during business hours. When the person you called listens to your message, he may not have access to a Rolodex, office files, or industry directory. Even if you think the person knows your phone number, do not take a chance. Leave your number and allow the person to get back to you right away.

YOUR OUTGOING MESSAGE

Whether the people calling your office love your voice mail or hate it depends on just two things. First, and most important, is how quickly you return telephone messages. Second, but also important, is the value they receive from your outgoing message.

Most people use their office voice mail just as they use their home answering machine. They record a single, all-purpose message and leave it on for months. At home there are three good reasons for vague answering machines messages: security, privacy, and technology. You wouldn't put a message on your answering machine that said, "we will be on vacation for two weeks." It would be an invitation to rob your home. And there is just no reason to tell people "We went to the movies and expect to be back at 11:30." Plus, the tape used in most home answering machines will wear out or break if you change your recording too frequently.

These factors do not hold in business. There is little security risk in telling callers that you are out of the office for the day. (If your voice-mail mailbox will be unused for an extended period of time, such as when you are out of the office for two weeks or more, consider forwarding calls to a secretary or co-worker rather than the voice-mail system. If a hacker comes across a message saying that you won't be using your mailbox for an extended period, the hacker may be tempted to "borrow" your mailbox for the duration.)

You may not want to tell every caller you are at a meeting and expect to return to your desk at 2:30, but at least let your callers know you plan to return phone calls around three o'clock that afternoon. Business voice-mail systems use digital recording for all messages. There are no moving parts to wear out or break down, even if you change your outgoing message several times a day.

Your voice-mail greeting must be specific and timely. Most voice-mail manufacturers recommend that a human being answer all telephone calls and transfer callers to a voice-mail mailbox only with their approval and only when they want to leave a message. Even though this is the ideal use for voice mail—as a message-taker only—not all companies choose to use it this way. If your company is using voice mail to reduce support staff, you may be forced to use voice mail to answer your calls when you are not at your desk.

When human beings answer your telephone calls, whether they are secretaries, receptionists, or co-workers, they tell your caller if you are out of the office for the day or if you have just stepped away from your desk. They route urgent calls to someone who might be able to help, and they make sure that the callers leave information, such as account names, that you will need when you return the call. Use voice mail to perform these same functions.

With a voice-mail system answering your telephone, you must plan for many factors in your greeting—you can't count on human intelligence (other than your own) to help your callers.

START WITH THE BASICS

All callers need to know your name and the name of your department. Don't forget to include these two important facts at the start of your voice-mail message. Voice-mail callers also need to know how to get back to the receptionist if their call has been misdirected.

If people from outside your company can reach your telephone directly (direct inward dial), you *must* include the name of your company in your voice-mail greeting. Often someone else's phone is forwarded to your extension. The first thing an outside caller will hear is a message with just your name, and the caller may think she has reached the wrong number.

Voice mail and answering machines are now so familiar that you don't have to ask your callers to "wait for the beep." Seconds are precious in a voice-mail greeting where you are trying to cram as much information as possible into the time allowed by your system and the attention span of your callers. Only mention the beep if it is unusual—if callers must wait for a second beep or if there will be a long pause after your message stops playing.

In your greeting you should also mention any other quirks of your voice-mail system, such as if it beeps every thirty seconds while recording a message.

A TALKING DESK?

It's amazing how many voice-mail greetings begin, "You have reached the desk of..." I'm not one of those people who has something against talking desks (I know what people mean when they say this), but some of your callers certainly will be. If for some reason you are uncomfortable speaking directly to your callers, it is more appropriate to say, "Hello. You have reached the voice-mail mailbox of..."

The best way to phrase your greeting, though, is as if you are talking directly to your caller. Voice mail is impersonal enough without increasing the distance between you and your caller by speaking as your voice-mail mailbox. If you are warm and friendly in your voice-mail greeting, people who have never spoken to you "live" will think of you as a warm and friendly person. The same will be true if you are calm and authoritative or bright and knowledgeable. This is really making technology work for you.

Remember that even though being personal is desirable, you should always be businesslike. Humor has its place—on your home answering machine. Your voice-mail greeting should reflect the professional image your company and department want to convey.

TELL CALLERS WHEN TO EXPECT A RETURN CALL

Voice mail can engender nightmares: the president of your company calls with a quick question on one of your projects. Your voice-mail message says, as it always does, "I'm not at my desk right now, but leave a message and I'll get right back to you." You are on vacation for the week, but the head of your company does not know that. As he leaves message after message he thinks less and less of you.

Change your message before you go on vacation, take a business trip, or leave the office for the day. If you are worried that callers will think less of you for taking a vacation, just say that you are out of the office—but let them know when you will be back.

Change your message too, before you go into a marathon meeting. Again, you do not have to say where you are if that makes you uncomfortable. Just let callers know when they can expect their calls to be returned. Many managers go from one meeting to another without much time in between to return calls. You may not be able to be specific about your schedule, but let your callers know why you are not there to answer their calls: "I will be in and out of meetings all day."

The important thing is to let your callers know when to expect a return call—and then to follow up on your promise. If you say you will return calls at 3 P.M. and then return calls first thing in the morning, the people who left messages for you will be disappointed, even if they didn't need to speak to you at 3 P.M. You will have created an expectation. At the very least, let callers know when you will be back at your desk so that they can call you again if they really need to speak with you.

If you plan to be out of the office for an extended period of time without checking your messages, keep in mind that all voice-mail systems have a limit on the number of voice-mail messages they can store at a given time (even if they claim they don't). Voice mail messages are stored much the same way data are stored on a computer. Each voice-mail system has only so much memory, which is sliced up differently depending on the system. In some voice-mail systems one busy mailbox can take up all the memory for the whole system. In others each mailbox is given only so much memory, and when that is full, no more messages can be recorded.

When this happens, the voice-mail system can do one of any number of things. Some play a "Sorry, this mailbox is full" message. Others return a busy signal or even hang up on your caller after your greeting is played. Your callers will be frustrated if you do not offer them options in your greeting and they cannot leave a message because your mailbox is full.

ASK CALLERS WHEN THEY NEED AN ANSWER

Knowing when a reply is needed helps you prioritize your callbacks. Delegate return calls to a member of your staff who can handle them. Most voice-mail systems let you forward a voice-mail message to someone else on the system and attach comments to the message. The process is as simple as pressing a few buttons on your telephone. If this feature wasn't part of your voice-mail basic training, look through your user's guide or ask the system administrator.

Forwarding calls to members of your staff can help you return calls and send information on time, but don't get into the habit of forwarding calls without first attaching a message of your own to them. Once you forward a voice-mail message the context is lost. Make sure that you summarize the transaction (especially who initiated the call) in your introduction to the forwarded message.

For example, the voice-mail message says, "Yeah, send your brochure to me at this address...." Now, is this a prospect giving you the brush-off? A prospect with a tight deadline and you lost the address the first time? A printer you have asked to bid on the brochure's next printing?

A simple "John, I promised this woman a brochure last week, but I lost her address. Can you treat this one with TLC?" can solve many problems before they start.

TELL CALLERS HOW TO REACH SOMEONE ELSE

One of the reasons people hate voice mail is its lack of options. You need to reach someone and it is urgent, but you have only two choices: leave a message or hang up. It doesn't have to be that way. If your voice-mail system lets callers dial another extension from your greeting (and all decent systems do), let your callers know who can help them when you are not available.

Some systems let you designate a "personal assistant." When the caller presses 0 during your greeting, the call goes to the department secretary or your assistant instead of the company switchboard. Even if your system does not have this feature, ask callers to "dial 327 and speak to my assistant Pat if you need help immediately." Designate different people for different questions so callers get to the person who can best help them. Have them talk to Pat to change an order and Terry to inquire about a shipping date.

Include information on how you can be reached in case of emergency or if you are out of the office. Some systems call you at a telephone number you program to deliver a message when the caller marks her call as urgent. This telephone number can be your beeper, your home phone number, or the regional office you are visiting that day. If your company's voice-mail system does not offer this feature, in your greeting leave your beeper number or a phone number where you can be reached in case of emergency.

There are very few voice-mail systems on the market that don't let callers reach the company receptionist by pressing zero during your recorded greeting. Most callers don't know this though, so it is up to you to mention it in your greeting. If you don't tell your callers exactly what your system is capable of, they will assume that it can do nothing else. You have stuck them with that awful choice between leaving a message and just hanging up.

TELL CALLERS WHAT INFORMATION YOU NEED

There are certain questions your callers frequently ask. And there is certain information you need to answer those questions. Do you need to know which version of a client contract they are referring to? Does your company operate on a fiscal year that is different from the calendar year? Make sure your greeting asks specifically for any information you cannot proceed without. The idea is to avoid having to call back just to get the information you need to answer a question. You want to call back with the answer.

If you include the answers to commonly asked questions during your greeting, you may be able to save the return phone call altogether. "The department meeting is at four o'clock today in the conference room." "Sales reports are due on the twentieth of the month." But have pity on other callers who have to listen to the whole greeting before they can leave a message. Keep the greeting brief. If a longer message would be helpful, direct callers to another mailbox where they can get all the details on the meeting or report.

CHANGE YOUR MESSAGE AS CIRCUMSTANCES WARRANT

Many voice-mail greetings invite callers to press zero to reach an operator. But after business hours when they press zero no one will answer. Don't tell callers they can reach an operator if they can't. Change the message when the operator goes home for the day.

Don't forget to change your message when you get out of a meeting or return from vacation. Out-of-date greetings make a bad impression. Get into the habit of changing your message regularly. For example, you could start each day by recording a new message that lets callers know if and when you will be available that day. This way you will always know your message is current, giving your callers valuable information.

What you put in your voice-mail greeting will depend on your job and the type of telephone calls you typically receive. Many people who change their messages every day include the day's date in the message. This is one way of letting callers know your message is up-to-date and that you pay attention to your voice mail. Some people even include a comment about the weather to warm up the coldness of a machine greeting.

Some people, by the nature of their jobs and the type of calls they get, have very long and complicated voice-mail greetings. Keep in mind that your callers can absorb only so much information over the telephone. Keep your message as short as you can. Don't ramble. If your voice-mail system gives you only so much time for your greeting, don't speak fast to get more information in. It is better to leave information out than to have a rushed message that your callers can't understand.

An excellent voice-mail greeting includes much information but delivers that information in a relaxed, unhurried voice. Each piece of information is delivered in as few words as possible while still remaining conversational.

SAMPLE GREETING

This all-purpose greeting is a good one to pattern your own voice-mail greeting on. Remember to meet the call-return deadline that you set.

"Hello. This is Terry Johnson in the order department of Big Company. I will be in meetings most of the day. The best time to reach me is after three this afternoon. If your call is urgent, please dial extension 327 and speak with my assistant Pat. Your call is important to me, and I look forward to speaking with you when I return your call at about four this afternoon."

MANAGEMENT ISSUES

Voice mail took managers by surprise. With no while-you-were-out messages littering employees' desks and with no frantic secretaries passing the word along, managers needed to create a new way to manage employees' telephone messages. Luckily, voice-mail system manufacturers made this fairly simple to do. Voice-mail systems usually can crank out reports on mailbox usage and other information about the system.

If you don't get reports on voice-mail system usage by your employees on a regular basis, ask for one. This report can be provided by your telecommunications department or the systems administrator for your voice-mail system. (Other departments that sometimes run the voice-mail system are the computing department, the personnel department, or the office manager.)

The first thing you should look for is any employee with many unlistened-to messages in his mailbox. In voice-mail system reports, new messages are usually listed separately from "stored" messages, or messages that have been listened to and saved. An employee with many new messages is probably not listening to and responding to his voice mail promptly and is probably making your customers or employees from other departments angry.

Another thing to look for is a mailbox with no activity over time. An unused voice-mail mailbox is a temptation for voice-mail hackers, who sometimes take over these mailboxes for their own use. If an employee legitimately does not need a voice-mail mailbox and does not use it, close it down for the sake of security.

If you call your employees regularly, you will have a good idea of what their voice-mail greetings are like and how frequently they change them. If you don't call your employees in the day-to-day workings of your department, call them for the purpose of listening to their outgoing messages.

Consider setting a department-wide outgoing message format. Because voice mail is still relatively new, few employees have training in the proper way to use it. You know what type of outgoing message works best for your department. Offer your employees a template message that they can customize. Set guidelines on how often outgoing messages should be changed and how quickly messages should be returned.

Some companies have a "same-day" rule for returning voice-mail messages. Others want employees to return calls within twenty-four hours. Depending on your business, it may be practical to wait as long as forty-eight hours, but make sure that you explain this policy to callers when they leave a message. Most callers expect their voice-mail messages returned in twenty-four hours.

Until everyone learns how to use voice mail effectively, many people will continue to hate it. But by using these principles, you can learn to love voice mail, not only for its convenience and time savings, but also for the new level of telephone effectiveness it offers.

Chapter 9

◆

Teleconferencing:

The Next Best Thing to Being There

"Focus on the people, not the technology."

—Charlotte Purvis

Teleconferencing may seem exotic, but it is not the sole domain of Fortune 500 companies with acoustic conference rooms and fancy equipment. If you have ever used the conference feature of your office telephone to connect a caller with another department and stayed on the line to mediate, you have participated in one type of teleconference.

Teleconferencing includes conference calls—voice-only conferences using telephones, speakerphones, or microphones and speakers— and video conferencing—sight and sound conferencing requiring special video equipment and telephone lines. It also includes audio-graphic conferencing (audio conferences enhanced with graphics transmitted by fax or another method) and data conferences.

Conference calls are by far the most common type of teleconference. For example, you are participating in a conference call when you stay on the line when transferring a telephone call. First, let's look more closely at what a conference call is all about and then move on to other types of teleconferencing.

KNOW YOUR TECHNOLOGY

A conference call blends your telephone effectiveness skills with your meeting skills. Depending on the technology you use, the mix of the skill groups will favor one or the other. The most basic type of conference call is where you use the conferencing feature of your company's telephone system to talk to several people in and out of your company at the same time. Everyone speaks on their own telephones.

The one thing you must know about using the conference feature of your telephone system is that the number of outside parties and inside lines that are practical to use during a conference are quite different from the numbers listed in the telephone system manual. Phone systems usually don't add amplification to conference calls. This means it quickly becomes difficult to hear what anyone is saying.

If your company frequently conducts large conferences by telephone, use a teleconferencing service. These services are available on a per-call basis from all the major long-distance telephone carriers and other smaller firms too. If your company is using teleconferencing services frequently, you might want to look into purchasing a teleconferencing bridge—a piece of hardware that is more sophisticated than the conferencing feature available from your phone system.

The next level of sophistication is to use a speakerphone while on your conference call. Use a speakerphone if you have several people at one location who need to interact together during the call or if several people at your company are participating in the conference call and your telephone system doesn't offer a conferencing feature.

Speakerphone technology gets better every day, but there are certain limitations that are expected, especially if you are not using state-of-the-art equipment. First, a conference call with a speakerphone is not a three-way or a ten-way conversation. Only one person can speak at a time. In many systems if one person interrupts another, she seizes the line, and no one is able to hear what the first person is saying. Even a loud noise, like a door slamming or a note-book dropping, can cause the system to switch to "listening" to someone other than the person who is speaking.

As the switching on speakerphones gets faster, it gets closer to sounding like a telephone conversation—where two people talk at the same time and both hear everything the other person said. To test how quickly a speakerphone switches, have a person at the other end of the line count to ten along with you at a rate you set. How many numbers do you hear? On many systems, whoever spoke first or loudest is the only one heard.

Slow switching between speakers also causes another problem, *clipping*. The speakerphone monitors all the lines and gives control to the line with the most noise on it. If someone on another line speaks, it switches control to that line. But listening, recognizing, and switching takes a split second and in that split second a sylla-ble or part of a syllable can be "clipped" off.

Our expectations of conference calls are based on the telephone, and our expectations of video conferencing are based on television. It is important to remember that in most cases, video conferencing doesn't look like the TV you see at home.

Television-like quality is possible, but it requires high-powered telecommunications links that are not only expensive but also must be specially installed, door-to-door, between the sites. In most cases, this high-quality video-conferencing service is available only between two or more sites designed only for this purpose. It may require trav-eling across town to the site of a video-conferencing service.

In most cases, the quality of the video conference is reduced so that it can be transmitted over more readily available telecommunica-tions links. Even these links are much more sophisticated than a regular telephone line. The motion on these transmissions may appear jerky, and you will notice a delay of several seconds between the time you say something and the time the person at the other end acknowledges.

Another video-conferencing option is a series of still images that are sent as quickly as a few seconds apart. The result is similar to looking at a slide show of still photographs taken with an auto-wind camera.

TELECONFERENCING: BUILDING ON MEETING SKILLS

The experts agree that poor meeting skills are magnified during a teleconference. Things you can get away with in a face-to-face meeting stop a teleconference cold. The first step toward an effective teleconference is to polish your meeting skills.

An agenda is essential for a teleconference. Ideally, the agenda should be prepared well in advance of the teleconference, and a copy should be sent to all participants. If there is no time to set an agenda before the teleconference, spend the beginning of the meeting developing one. Other materials (charts, diagrams, maps) should also be sent ahead of time to all the participants. These visual aids help focus the participants' attention. They are especially important in long meetings.

Charlotte Purvis, a teleconferencing consultant and head of Purvis Communications, Inc., in Durham, North Carolina, suggests using twenty-five percent more visual material in a conference call than you would in a face-to-face meeting. In a face-to-face meeting, visuals enhance the message. In a conference call, they must substitute for your presence.

"Face-to-face meetings are more spontaneous," says Purvis. "You can draw on a chalkboard. For a teleconference you want to think ahead of everything they would get if you were on site."

For a conference call that will last more than an hour, Purvis recommends that these materials include biographical sketches and photographs of the speakers. She has found that participants interact more and listen better during a conference call when they can associate a face with the voice. If the participants have never met in person, a photograph helps bridge the gap.

Of course, in a face-to-face meeting you rely on "visuals" for more than charts and graphs and knowing what the speaker looks like. Eye contact lets you know if participants are paying attention, if they understand what is being said, and if they wish to ask a question. In a conference call, you must make accommodations for the lack of visual feedback. Instead of looking for feedback, you must ask for it and listen for it.

No teleconference should go more than ten minutes without some kind of shift, warns Purvis. Use this shift between speakers or topics to ask for feedback. Keep a list of the names of the participants in front of you as a visual cue—to replace looking at the faces of people sitting around a conference table.

The way Charlotte Purvis sees it, these special requirements of a teleconference call make it "more polite" than a regular meeting. Because different types of teleconferencing equipment have different features, the protocol for the teleconference is set by the leader or a moderator who is familiar with the system. These simple rules will make your conference call more effective:

◆ One person speaks at a time. Wait for the speaker to finish before you start to talk.

◆ Identify yourself when you speak.

◆ Address questions to specific individuals.

◆ The leader must be sure no one person overwhelms the discussion.

◆ Plan to join the conference call, or call in to the conferencing service, three to five minutes before it is scheduled to start. Conference leaders should call in even earlier.

When you participate in a face-to-face conference, you walk into a room, someone closes the door, and you are pretty sure you won't be disturbed until the meeting is over. When you participate in a conference call, it is up to you to "close the door" on disruptions before the meeting starts. Close the door of your office, put your phone on do-not-disturb, or tell your assistant or secretary to hold your calls. If the conference call will be a long one, use a headset to prevent the discomfort that comes with a long telephone call. If you can't get your hands on a headset, borrow a speakerphone. In a pinch, you can use the speaker on your telephone, although these are usually not as high quality as a specialized speakerphone.

During a conference call, you make an impression with both the quality of your voice and the quality of the telephone technology you use. In a video conference, your appearance is very important.

As far as your appearance is concerned, preparing for a video conference is the same as preparing for a television appearance. For example, wearing white may give you a washed out look. Women should be careful of spots of makeup. Reflections on your glasses can have an impact on your image. If you participate in many video conferences (or also appear frequently on television) consider having your eye-care professional treat your glasses to prevent glare on camera.

During a video conference, it is important to balance the amount of time the camera is focused on participants with the amount of time that is spent on documents, product demonstrations, and other visuals.

"Try to avoid 'talking heads,' where the camera is only focused on people talking," says Purvis. "When you watch the news, you don't want to see thirty minutes of Peter Jennings—or thirty minutes of visuals. Like the news, your video conference should strive for a balance."

A video-conferencing system is a big investment. If your company has its own system, training or orientation should be available from the video-conferencing staff, the telecommunications department, or the training staff. If your company rents a teleconferencing room from an outside company, that company has experts available to train you in effective techniques for video conferencing.

Still-frame video is totally overlooked but is effective at adding visuals even on an impromptu basis. Also consider audio-graphic conferences. An audio-graphic conference pairs a conference call with graphics transmitted by fax or by special equipment during the conference.

WHEN TO TELECONFERENCE

Teleconferences cannot replace face-to-face meetings. Meetings have many functions, and often distributing information or getting input from many people is just a small part of their purpose. A meeting that serves in part to build camaraderie or team spirit might not work well as a teleconference. Teleconferencing is also not appropriate when sensitive issues need to be discussed or when delicate negotiations must be made.

Teleconferences work best when all the participants know each other well. Like a telephone call between old friends, the better you know each other, the less you rely on visual cues to understand what is being said. Many companies look to teleconferencing to save money on travel costs, but a teleconference does more than save on travel. And in cases where a teleconference is not appropriate, the costs of a harmful teleconference are more than the travel costs of an effective meeting.

Teleconferences work best

- ◆ to replace a repetitive call such as when a sales manager makes the same phone call to each of ten salespeople;

- ◆ to give people the benefit of hearing other people's questions;

- ◆ to take the place of a routine or regularly scheduled meeting;

- ◆ to convey information when something is too urgent for mail—even overnight mail;

◆ to accommodate people when they complain of being burned out from traveling;

◆ to help people when they feel isolated because everyone is traveling so much they can't keep in touch;

◆ to set the agenda before a big meeting; and

◆ to follow-up and get feedback after a big meeting.

WHEN YOU ARE THE CONFERENCE LEADER

If you are to moderate a teleconference and you have never participated in one before, arrange to participate in one. If your company uses its own equipment in-house, this may mean sitting in on a conference run by a co-worker. If your company uses a teleconferencing service, contact the service company and ask to sit in on a demonstration meeting.

Even if you have participated in teleconferences before, as a first-time leader, you should call your service company or vendor. The company can provide you with a list of features and services. There are so many features available, chances are the feature that will help your conference run smoother is there waiting for you to ask for it. Talk to someone in reservations and tell her the goal of your meeting. This person will be able to tell you which features and services will help you meet those goals.

When you are comfortable with the teleconferencing system you will use, schedule the conference with your conference company or reserve time on the company system. Next, notify the participants and distribute materials to them. If your company's image is on the line, such as at a press conference or stockholders' meeting, have a rehearsal for both the people and the technology.

When you are the leader, phone in to the conference earlier than you would if you were just a participant. Purvis recommends calling in five to ten minutes before the conference is scheduled to begin.

With a feeling for how a teleconference is similar to a face-to-face meeting and a knowledge of how the technology limits it, you will be able to run a teleconference that is both successful and effective.

When you are the conference call leader, it is very important to ask for feedback, both on the content of the conference and on the process of how the meeting is being run. As we saw earlier, asking for feedback and participation is very important to a successful teleconference, especially a conference call. As the leader, you also need feedback on how the information in the conference is coming across. With this feedback you can adjust your own techniques accordingly, both to make the current conference go smoothly and to improve future calls that you moderate.

Chapter 10

Using Telephone Technology:

How to Make Technology Work for You—Not Against You

"Many jobs are changing because of technology advances, and a highly competent occupant on any rung of the ladder may become obsolete through failure to move with the times."

—Dr. Laurence J. Peter *(Why Things Go Wrong)*

Telephone technology includes facsimile machines, automated attendants, telecommunications software, and a host of other gadgetry. It seems that every few years a new wave of telephone technology sweeps the business world. Office policies and business etiquette haven't always kept up with the new technologies though. With a little insight and some common sense, you can be the master of telephone technology. Today's telephone may be more complicated than yesterday's simple dial and receiver, but used correctly, it is a more powerful tool.

AUTOMATED ATTENDANTS

If you have ever called a company and heard a recorded announcement welcoming you and asking you to press an extension, to press zero for the operator, or to "hold the line and an operator will be with you shortly," you have been greeted by an automated attendant.

Survey after survey shows that automated attendants are the most despised piece of business equipment around. So why do businesses use them? Automated attendants can't compare to the service offered by an excellent receptionist, but they are superior—and a lot cheaper—than the service offered by a poor one. Whether companies are motivated by the savings an automated attendant offers, or they have found the device to be the best solution to a chronic problem with bad receptionists, it is clear that automated attendants have become a part of business life.

There is a lot of confusion in the terminology used for voice-processing systems such as automated attendants and voice mail. Most people use the term *voice mail* to mean any recording they hear over the telephone. Actually voice mail refers only to the automated message-taking function of a voice-processing system. *Automated attendant* is the proper name for the function that answers and routes calls. A company buys a system that includes both these functions, but they can be used separately.

Even if you are one of the many who hates automated attendants, you can use a few simple techniques to help you get along with them better.

OTHER COMPANIES

When you know the extension of the person you are calling, you can skip the long instruction and selection menus, the wait for the operator, and even the initial greeting. Press the extension of the person you are trying to reach as soon as you hear a recorded voice. Occasionally, using an automated attendant requires special instructions, such as entering the extension after a beep or pressing the pound key (#) before entering the extension. If you enter the extension incorrectly or too soon, you will just be dumped back at the initial greeting and will have lost only a few seconds.

If you call another company and are greeted by an automated attendant, there is not much you can do if you are not prepared.

With so many of these devices around, the best thing to do is to become an avid collector of people's telephone extensions.

Get into the habit of asking for a person's extension when you get his telephone number. Add extensions to your records—in your phone book or on your Rolodex—and jot them on business cards when you receive them, if an extension isn't printed already. Having telephone extensions turns automated attendants into time-savers; without them, they are time-wasters.

This suggestion is so simple, but it makes the world of difference. Asking for extensions should be as much a part of your telephone routine as asking for an area code. Once again, the key to automated attendants is knowing the extension number of every person you call.

If you are calling a specific person but don't know the extension, press zero as soon as you hear the recording. This transfers you immediately to the operator and eliminates your having to listen to the entire recorded greeting.

YOUR COMPANY

There is much you can do to make your company's automated attendant work more effectively for you and your callers.

◆ Use the automated attendant on "back door" telephone lines— those lines not used by first-time callers or potential customers.

◆ Present the automated attendant as a benefit or a valuable service to your employees, frequent customers, and suppliers. Point out that the automated attendant will give them instant access to the party they wish to reach. They will no longer need to wait for a receptionist to pick up the phone and transfer the call.

◆ Don't expect an automated attendant to replace personal assistance from a company receptionist or a departmental secretary. If they wish to, callers should always be able to reach a human being. (After hours and on holidays, the instructions in your greeting should change to reflect the fact that there is no human available to handle calls directed to the operator.)

◆ Don't surprise callers with a new automated attendant. Write letters to your contacts explaining the new system and giving them your extension.

◆ Keep recorded greetings short.

◆ Limit menus to three or fewer options at a time. Too many options will confuse callers.

◆ Always give the choice first and then tell callers which button to push. For example, say, "For sales, press one. For accounts payable, press two." Don't say, "Press one for sales...."

◆ Put menu options in the order of popularity. If most callers want the sales department, put that option first. If most callers want customer service, put that first. When you first install the system you may have to guess what choices are the most popular. (Ask your receptionist. He probably has a good idea where most calls go.) After the system has been running for a while, reports generated by the system will tell you which menu option is the most popular choice. Reprogram your system to make it first.

◆ Put menu choices in number order, with no gaps if possible. If you move sales from option three to the first option offered, make sure you change its number too. Automated attendants are confusing enough without hearing, "For sales, press seven. For customer service, press three...."

◆ Have new business cards and stationery printed that include your telephone extension in addition to your telephone number.

AUTOMATED GREETING

If you answer thirty or more calls each day, you may find yourself getting hoarse, or at least less enthusiastic, by early afternoon. A device designed for company receptionists and customer service representatives can help you greet your last caller with the same perkiness that you greeted your first. The device is call an automated greeting or personal announcer.

First thing in the morning, you record your greeting on the device. Then, depending on the device and your telephone system, you either pick up the phone and press a button or the device answers the call automatically. In both cases your greeting is played to the caller. Because the greeting is recorded in your voice, few (if any) callers know that you had help answering their call.

If your greeting is long, and you answer many calls, this device can help you sound calm and professional even on the most hectic day.

INTERACTIVE VOICE RESPONSE

Another voice-processing technology, related to automated attendants and voice mail, is interactive voice response, often known as IVR. This sophisticated technology links telephones to a computer database. The most common example of IVR is banking by telephone. You call a special number at the bank and enter your account number and perhaps an ID number. Then you follow a menu and can hear your account balance, the amount of the last check deposited and other information.

Interactive voice response is helpful anytime you would like to give callers access to complex information and relieve your staff from answering repetitive questions. If you have ever wished you could give your callers limited access to computer information over the telephone, IVR is the technology for you.

FACSIMILE

If automated attendants are the least popular business technology, facsimile—or fax—is surely one of the most popular. Indeed, the biggest problem with fax machines, it seems, is not having one. There are several things you can do to make your fax more effective:

◆ Small type, and certain typefaces, don't transmit clearly. Use the largest type possible on your faxes—it should be at least ten-point type. Dot-matrix printing, for example does *not* fax well. Try to avoid it. Laser printing, however, does fax well.

Adobe Systems, a computer graphics company, tested several typefaces and rated the following as the best for faxing in this order: *Palatino; Helvetica; ITC Bookman, New Century Schoolbook; Courier.*

1. Palatino
2. **Helvetica**
3. ITC Bookman
4. New Century Schoolbook
5. Courier

◆ A cover sheet adds privacy to your fax message. Letters come in envelopes and phone calls are heard by only one person, but fax messages are there for anyone to read. The cover sheet gives your fax message an "envelope" so its contents can't be easily read by everyone who handles it.

◆ Call before or after sending a fax. Many companies have not yet worked the bugs out of their fax distribution system. If the recipient is expecting the fax or knows it has arrived, there is a better chance that she will actually receive it.

◆ Don't believe everything your fax machine says. Some machines have a display or a tone that "confirms" the fax has arrived at the receiving machine. However, this confirmation does not mean your fax has really reached its intended recipient or that the entire fax has been printed out at the receiving machine. Many things can go wrong, even if you get a confirmation. If it is important, check to make sure that the fax has arrived.

◆ Faxes printed on thermal paper are delicate. Never put a fax on a heater, radiator, or in direct sunlight. Thermal paper reacts to the heat of the fax machine typehead by turning black. It will do the same on your windowsill, blacking out all that was printed there.

Faxes printed on high-quality thermal paper last about five years if they are keep away from heat and direct light. Cheap fax paper fades more quickly—in a few years, or even a few months.

If you need a permanent copy of the fax—for legal reasons or for storing the fax in a permanent file—or if you are not sure of the quality of your paper, make a photocopy.

Faxes printed on a plain paper fax machine have none of these problems. They have the same characteristics as a document printed out on a bubble jet or laser printer (depending on what method is used to print them). The trade-off is that plain paper faxes jam more often than thermal paper machines. Expect your plain paper fax to jam as frequently as your photocopier does. (Both have something to do with the quality of the paper.)

◆ The big advantage fax messages have over telephone messages is that they don't necessarily interrupt your work. If someone is going to call you back with a quick confirmation, approval, or brief message, have him fax it to you instead of calling. You handle the message when it's most convenient for you, not whenever the call happens to come in.

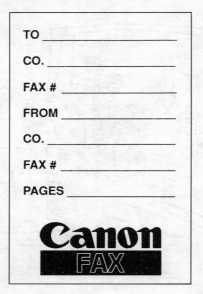

THE COVER SHEET

The idea behind a fax cover sheet is that the person you send the fax to should have enough information to

◆ determine if he has received all the pages sent,

◆ know who to contact if he has not received the complete transmission,

◆ reply to your fax by fax immediately, and

◆ call you immediately by telephone to acknowledge receipt of the fax or ask more questions.

You can shorten the amount of time it takes to send a fax by minimizing vertical lines framing empty space, such as in borders and boxes. A thin line around your cover page looks pretty, but it forces the fax machine to go edge to edge on every line. Let your stationery designer know this.

Federal law says that all your faxes must identify the sender, either with a cover sheet or header/footer that gives the recipient your name and fax number. Make sure an I.D. is programmed into your fax machine. Even if you always send a cover sheet, remember that cover sheets can get separated from the rest of the fax.

This is another good reason to make sure your fax I.D. appears on every page. Every so often faxes will get collated incorrectly, and page one of one fax winds up with page two of another fax. If your fax number appears on every page, the recipient of your missorted fax can contact you to send the fax again. Without identification on every page, she may just have to throw away an intriguing middle page of a fax because she doesn't know who sent it.

FACSIMILE COVER SHEET

[YOUR COMPANY NAME OR LOGO]

TO: _____

COMPANY: _____

FAX NUMBER: _____

FROM: _____

COMPANY: _____

FAX NUMBER: _____

TELEPHONE NUMBER: _____

This fax has _____ pages, including this cover sheet.

FAX/MODEMS

If you work at a PC and find yourself printing letters and then faxing them, you may want to consider using a fax/modem. These fax
devices come on a PC board that slides into one of the empty slots
in your PC (IBM and compatible microcomputers) or are attached
to the back of your computer with a cable. As the name suggests,
these devices function both as a fax machine (of sorts) and as a
modem.

Software that comes with the fax/modem lets you convert a text (or graphics) file in your computer into a fax-friendly format. It then faxes it to another fax machine or another fax/modem-equipped computer.

Fax/modems cost about one hundred dollars—or less. They can be very simple or quite sophisticated. Either way, the fax/modem will cost less than a fax machine with the same features.

Fax/modems can save on paper if you fax many letters or memos, but mostly they save you time and money. If you need to find a fax machine in another department or on another floor—or if you must wait on line to use the company fax machine—a fax/modem can give you a significant time savings.

Fax/modems are also convenient if you often send the same fax message to many people. The fax/modem can be programmed to send the faxes automatically—even to send them after business hours to save on phone costs.

All fax/modems must convert your computer files into faxable form before they can be sent. This process takes about as long as printing the document. Some fax/modem software converts more quickly than others, just as some printers print more quickly than others.

What a fax/modem won't let you do is take something not already in your computer, such as a newspaper article or a letter from someone else, and turn it into faxable form. For this you need to add a scanner (or use a regular fax machine).

Fax/modems are also helpful for receiving faxes. You can pre-view faxes you receive before printing them out. In some cases you can just deal with the information on your computer screen and don't have to print the fax at all.

Keep in mind that a fax/modem has the same telephone line requirements as a fax machine or a modem. If these devices don't work hooked up to your office telephone system (and they don't on many), you will need a special analog line to use your fax/modem at your desk.

FAX-ON-DEMAND

If you receive many telephone calls where people simply ask you to fax them information, or if you have members of your department whose job it is to send faxes to people who request them, you may benefit from a fax-on-demand system. A fax-on-demand system automates the sending of faxes that have previously been stored in the system.

For example, one of your customers may call the system looking for a technical schematic of one of your products. The customer calls a special telephone number and is greeted by a recording, much like an automated attendant. The greeting leads the caller to the information he wants. ("For schematics, press one. For price lists, press two.") Or the greeting may prompt new users to ask for a listing of all available documents.

The caller enters the code number of the document he wants on his touch-tone keypad. Then the system asks him to enter the number of his fax machine. Within seconds, the fax-on-demand system sends the document to the caller's fax machine. In another variation, you can ask callers to call from a fax machine. Instead of calling them back, the system simply sends the fax to the caller's machine on the same call. This one-call variety of fax-on-demand will save your company money by eliminating the second call that you pay for, but it is less convenient for your customers.

CELLULAR TELEPHONES

Cellular telephone technology has become so advanced in the last few years that there is little reason to treat a cellular call differently from any other telephone call—with two main exceptions. The first exception is driving safety. If you use a cellular telephone while driving, driving safely takes priority over using the telephone effectively. Don't take notes, and use hands-free options whenever possible.

The other, and clearly less important exception, is the cost. Cellular telephone calls are not as expensive as they used to be, but you still always pay something for the call—even if the other person calls you. For this reason, you should give out the number of your cellular phone sparingly. And whether you made the call or someone called you, you should use time-saving tactics to keep the call as short as possible.

HEADSETS

Do you end the day with a sore neck? Sore shoulders? Do your ears burn? Is your arm cramped? All these problems are symptoms of having spent too much time on the phone. You probably can't solve these problems by cutting down on phone time, but you can take a cue from telephone operators and telemarketers and use a headset. For years, headsets were regarded as tools for receptionists. Because anyone wearing a headset was viewed as support staff, managers were reluctant to wear them.

Headset manufacturers are aware of this feeling. They have come out with new lines of "executive headsets" with an emphasis on personal choice and appearance. More and more are using the new style headsets, but you still may encounter some surprised looks when someone walks into your office when you are wearing one.

Stockbrokers were among the first professionals to use headsets. And of course the headset has become part of the stereotype of the Hollywood agent. The Hollywood influence especially has put headset-wearing professionals in front of the public through their appearance in movies. The problem is no longer just people thinking you are a receptionist, but also that people may think a headset is too glamorous for a mere manager.

But it is probably worth it. Not only does a headset cut down on those phone-related aches and pains, it helps you get more work done if you need two hands to take notes, access a computer, or search through files while on the phone. A study performed by research from H.B. Maynard & Company for Plantronics (a headset manufacturer) showed that salespeople, travel agents, technical field sales support people, and stockbrokers were forty-three percent more productive when they used a headset, depending on how fast their computer was and how fast they typed.

CONTROLLING COSTS
The most important thing to do to control recurring telephone costs is to choose the correct long-distance service for your company's usage. That is, not just the best long-distance company but the best

service or plan the company offers. There is no easy way out of making this decision. In some large companies there is an employee whose only job is to constantly evaluate the company's phone usage and find the best long-distance service for that usage pattern.

COMMON COST-CUTTING TECHNIQUES

In most companies, the most effective telephone cost-cutting techniques (choosing a long distance service, auditing equipment charges from your local telephone company) probably will be the responsibility of the telecommunications department, purchasing department, or office manager. But there are a few things you can do within your own department to cut down on telephone costs:

◆ Set a personal calls policy. Many managers feel a policy of no personal calls at all is too restrictive. You probably will want to restrict international calls because they can be quite expensive. Domestic long-distance calls are another story. In many cases, a long distance call costs no more than a local call. Time wasted on personal calls should be the issue rather than the cost of the calls themselves. Whatever policy you set, be sure it is explained clearly when an employee joins your department.

◆ Make sure employees know that someone always pays for "toll-free" 800 or 888 number calls. This is important if your company has more than one location. Employees may call between locations on the company's toll-free numbers, thinking those calls are really free from toll charges, not just free of charge to the people who are making them. In some cases, your company may be paying more for the 800 call than they would for a call on their regular telephone number. Make sure employees use the least-expensive method of calling between company locations, whether it's a tie-line, a regular telephone number, or a toll-free number.

If your employees know that your company pays for toll-free calls, they will be less tempted to ask their friends and relatives to call them at work using your toll-free number. Explain to all employees that your company pays for the call whether the employee makes the call or someone else calls them on your toll-free number.

Many companies use a "call-accounting" system to give their managers a breakdown of telecommunications cost by department. If you don't already receive this report monthly, ask your system administrator or accounting department for a copy. Be on the lookout for sharp increases in the amount of time or money your department spends. Is there a reasonable explanation for it? You may have been working on a big project that can account for the extra telephone calls.

If your call volume has shot up without explanation, consider that your telephone system may have been "hacked" by outsiders who are stealing telephone time from your company. Report unexplained call volume (or cost) spikes to your system administrator.

Your company's call-accounting system is a good way to put a lid on excessive phone use by your department. If you suspect your department is abusing its telephone privileges, ask for a call-accounting report by extension. This will tell you who spends the most time on the telephone and what number they are calling. Many managers find that just the threat of being held accountable for telephone calls made puts an end to telephone privilege abuse.

Make sure that your employees know that a call-accounting system just gives you a telephone bill-like report of their telephone calls and how much they cost. Some employees confuse call accounting with call monitoring, where managers listen in to employees' calls. Some union contracts forbid call monitoring, and a federal law against call monitoring has been pending in Congress for some time. It's hard to imagine the circumstances that would give an employee a legitimate complaint against call accounting.

CONTACT MANAGEMENT SOFTWARE

If you are using the telephone frequently and effectively, you may find your Rolodex is bulging with names and telephone numbers, and that your desk is littered with small scraps of paper from notes you took while on the phone. There is software available to help you organize this mess. This software was first designed for telephone salespeople, but now people with many types of job titles use contact management software to help organize their calls and call information.

Three of the most popular brands of contact management software are Goldmine from Goldmine Software, Act! from Symantec, and TeleMagic from Remote Control. There are many other kinds of contact management software available, and some may be more suited to your particular needs than others.

In general, contact management software creates a record for the people you call. This record includes important information about each person, including name, address, telephone number, extension, products or services they are interested in, and other pertinent information, some of which you can customize to your needs. The record also includes a place to take notes during a telephone call (or to transcribe notes you took by hand after the call is over).

With the push of a few keys or with a few clicks of the mouse, the software also notes if you promise to call the person at a later date. It schedules the appointment and may even remind you by sounding an alarm and popping the person's record onto your computer screen when the time comes.

With all the information about a particular person in front of you, you will know what you discussed last time, if the subject of this call is consistent with the person's previous call, and even the name of the person's children to help you make small talk.

Having all this information on hand also lets you sort your database of contacts in many ways. Let's say you are planning a business trip to the Southwest. Sort your database to find all your contacts in that area and plan other meetings while you are there. Is your company having a big sale on widgets? Sort your database for prospects who have shown an interest in widgets. Even better, create a list of those who have objected to the price.

Many systems will let you take that list and automatically dial through it without touching your keypad. You'll need a modem attached to your telephone and computer, but with this set-up you can speed through a long list of calls in no time.

A FEW WORDS ABOUT THE INTERNET

Using electronic mail (e-mail) or the Internet is a little like writing a letter, a little like using the telephone, and a lot like nothing else.

E-mail is most like the telephone in the speed with which you respond to messages. Responding to e-mail is similar to responding to your voice-mail messages.

The basic rule for both e-mail and the telephone is to respond as quickly as possible after receiving the message. You should respond within a few hours to anything time-sensitive and within twenty-four hours to almost any message.

It's okay to let things go up to three days if you are extremely busy and the message is obviously not urgent or time-sensitive—but that is the absolute limit. Of course, you don't have to respond to messages that are just for your information or don't request a reply.

Computer folks are big on rules. For e-mail—direct computer-based communication between two people—the rules are as relaxed as you get. Depending on your relationship to the person you are sending the e-mail to, it can be as informal as a handwritten note you might leave on someone's desk or as formal as a professionally written sales letter you send to prospects.

When you get into electronic bulletin boards, Internet "chat" rooms, or discussion groups, the rules are pretty strict and vary slightly from site to site. For example, the response time for messages or questions posted on the Internet usually goes much longer than the three-day rule for e-mail. One universal rule is that you should use upper- and lowercase letters just as you would in written communication. Comments written in all capital letters are used to symbolize yelling. SO DON'T DO IT UNLESS YOU WANT PEOPLE TO THINK YOU'RE SCREAMING!

In many Internet chat rooms "emoticons" are used to show that you are saying something with a smile or that a comment has made you laugh. The basic smile is :-) (tilt your head, chin to the right to see the smiley face).

Each electronic meeting place can use its own shorthand, however. In Compuserve forums many people use <g> for "grin" to mean the same thing as :-). Some people get very creative with their emoticons, using them to represent everything from laughing out loud to a slight cringe.

Before you plunge in on the Internet, listen in briefly (but very briefly or people will accuse you of "lurking") and use the resources posted for new participants. Look for the FAQ file. This stands for Frequently Asked Questions. Reading this file first may save you from looking like an idiot. At least it will save you from waiting three days for a response to a question that had been answered by the group months or years before.

USING A TDD

A Telecommunications Device for the Deaf or TDD lets deaf and hearing-impaired people communicate through the telephone network. A basic TDD has a keyboard and a screen. Messages are typed on the keyboard and received on the screen.

With the passage of the Americans with Disabilities Act (ADA), TDDs have become much more common in business. If you need to communicate by TDD, you should know several things.

First, TDDs have their own etiquette and lingo. Most TDDs let only one party talk at a time, making them more like a walkie-talkie or CB radio than a telephone. Also, typing takes a lot longer than talking. For these two reasons a TDD is not used like a "visual telephone." There are special shorthand terms used and a different flow to the call.

The rhythm of TDD conversations is different from phone conversations. For example, to save time several questions may be asked at once before "GA", for go ahead, is typed to request a reply.

If you are not an experienced TDD user and you think you will be using the TDD frequently, ask to observe or read conversations between experienced users. Keep in mind that saving the paper that the TDD conversation is printed on is considered rude. You will need permission from both parties to "listen in" on their conversation in this way.

There are other alternatives for communicating with deaf and hearing-impaired people over the telephone. One alternative is a relay service, which is available through many long-distance companies. With a relay service, you speak to an operator, just as you would to the person you are calling. The operator types your message into a TDD and sends it to the person you want to communicate with. That person's response is sent by TDD to the operator and spoken by the operator over the telephone to you.

Yet another alternative to the TDD is a fax machine. For business-to-business communications, this can be an excellent solution for communicating with deaf or hearing-impaired people. After all, just about every company has a fax machine. For communicating with customers at home, though, this works only if the person you are trying to reach also has a fax machine.

If you haven't given thought to how you would communicate with a deaf or hearing-impaired customer, it is time to start thinking now. The ADA requires most businesses to treat customers equally. If you offer services by telephone to hearing customers, you should have equivalent services for deaf and hearing-impaired customers.

MOVING WITH THE TIMES

Your company's telecommunications manager comes to a meeting with a great idea for a new gizmo for your company. She goes on and on about gigs and baud and throughput. You listen but eventually become drowsy. You see no reason your department needs this gadget, but how do you know you are not missing out on the next big thing? Or maybe you got stuck with buying telecommunications equipment for your company and salespeople's presentations leave you just as woozy.

To be fair, telecommunications managers and salespeople have all types of backgrounds. Not all of them are so wrapped up in the technology that they forget to say what the latest gizmo is good for. But it seems all too common that telecommunications folk "sell" using features instead of the benefits for your department or company. Don't be shy. Pin them down. Ask them what the device can do for your department. If they answer with a list of more features (bytes, RAM, call capacity) ask for an example of how the technology has been used successfully at another company.

In most cases, the look of understanding on their faces will be immediate. (And chances are it will soon follow on your own as they finally explain what this thing can do for you.) Sometimes you will see a small look of pity flicker across their faces, but that's okay. Knowing how to get technical people to speak your language is the best way to make sure you don't miss out on the next technology that's as popular and useful as facsimile or the Internet.

The telephone is your most powerful business tool. Not only does it bring the world right to your desk, but it also lets you talk back to it. The typical business telephone call is brief, but you should not judge its importance by its length. It is through telephone calls that we build relationships, forge alliances, and sell products and services.

Using the telephone effectively means planning your telephone calls before you make them, taking notes on each call, and eliminating telephone tag by leaving messages that say when you will be available to receive calls or finding out the best time to call back.

By using the techniques in this book, you will view new telephone technologies such as voice mail, automated attendants, and teleconferencing as tools for telephone effectiveness and increased productivity instead of roadblocks to communication. Now that you have added business telephone skills to the social telephone skills you have had for years, you will find that the telephone no longer seems to be an interruption to important tasks. It has become a means to accomplish those tasks more effectively.

INDEX